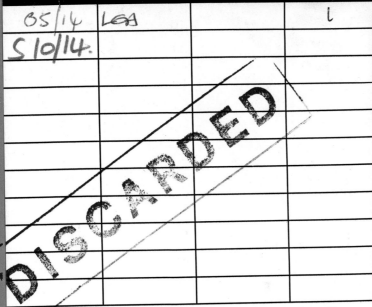

Dinner's ON!

Dinner's ON!

BARRY LEWIS

PHOTOGRAPHY BY MYLES NEW

Harper
Collins

For Nan, my best friend, forever missed.

HarperCollins*Publishers*
77–85 Fulham Palace Road,
Hammersmith, London W6 8JB

www.harpercollins.co.uk

First published by HarperCollins*Publishers* 2014

1 3 5 7 9 10 8 6 4 2

Text © Barry Lewis 2014
Photography © Myles New 2014

Barry Lewis asserts the moral right to be identified as the author of this work

A catalogue record of this book is available from the British Library

Food styling: Joanna Farrow and Rebecca Rauter
Props styling: Tony Hutchinson

ISBN   978-0-00-754459-2

Printed and bound by South China Printing Company Ltd

CONTENTS

⚡

This is a surreal but extremely proud moment for me – introducing my very own cookbook.

A few years ago I would have thought you were bonkers if you had told me this was going to happen. Back then I couldn't cook anything; I had absolutely no confidence in the kitchen or interest in food (other than eating it!) – I was a cookery virgin, so to speak. If you don't believe me, check out my very first recipe video attempt: 'Poached egg on toast'.

My partner Becky (affectionately known as Mrs Barry) would always have dinner on the table for me when I returned home from work, and when she wasn't around I'd just survive on microwave meals or order a takeaway. My cooking epiphany came soon after I bought Mrs Barry a camcorder for Christmas. A few days later I was watching television and saw Jamie Oliver poaching an egg. I thought to myself 'I can give that a go' so I borrowed Mrs Barry's camera, set up a YouTube channel and, with the help of some basic editing software, My Virgin Kitchen was born. I only intended to make a few videos at first to motivate myself, but when I realised I could inspire others it started to become an addiction! There was never a secret business plan; it has always been about my journey in the kitchen, recording my memories and experiences along the way. I have tried to learn as much as possible, and I'm happy to say that I have had a huge helping of laughter too, which I think is extremely important – laugh and learn folks.

When I realised that cooking could be fun, it gave me the confidence to keep going. Don't be afraid to make mistakes; learn from them! Soon enough you will be adding that sprinkling of creativity – 'next time I might just try adding some different herbs' – and once you get that same buzz from cooking that I do, you will be well on your way. That's my aim for this book: to introduce you to my world by getting you to have fun in the kitchen by making great food and creating some happy memories too.

Food really does make memories. I've absolutely loved getting Phoebe (my eldest daughter who features in some of the beauty and the beast style photos throughout the book) in the kitchen with me learning basic cooking skills. More recently my younger daughter Chloe has been getting involved too and Phoebe is passing on what we've learnt – cooking has brought us closer together.

There have been some pretty cool experiences to date on this journey too. Jamie inspired me in a kind of accidental way, then I just kept on making the videos. I made a homemade Big Mac that I thought was pretty funny as I was wearing an afro wig, so Tweeted Jamie and, amazingly, he replied:

@myvirginkitchen good lad good job there's something cool about it...keep it up jamie o

We shared a few tweets back and forth after that. I started to notice that my channel was growing, and it was turning into more than a hobby so when I heard Jamie was launching his FoodTube channel and wanted me to play a part in it, I decided to take a big step. I took a break from my job in the construction industry to concentrate on sharing my story and inspiring more people full time. Things went a little mad after the live launch show and my story hit local, national and international news. Getting to meet and be part of Jamie Oliver's network has been incredible, very inspirational and I have learnt a lot. He has

Introduction

been incredibly supportive whenever I've needed advice. I have also had the chance to do some fun stuff like attempting to make a giant vegan marshmallow for Bryan Adams, blowing up watermelons with my mind on television and cooking in a hotel room using an iron! I have discovered that spatulas are AMAZING (please don't ask me why, they just are. I have declared my love for them a few times throughout this book). I have opened my mind to new flavours and tastes: I now absolutely love beetroot, tomatoes and olives, and rave to Mrs Barry about passion fruit and mangoes. In the past the only discussion I'd have about food is 'why are there gherkins in McDonalds burgers?' I never thought I could be this passionate about food. Of course, sharing your kitchen and a certain element of your life online can make things fun – when some chap from Brazil notices you have changed your kettle, things do get surreal! I hope this is just the start of it and I'm so glad to have you on board!

A popular question is what's my favourite recipe? To be honest, I have several – the Chicken & Bacon Caesar Salad (see page 29), BBQ Pulled Pork Ciabattas (see page 112) and the Lemon Poppy Seed Muffins (page 194) are all up there. But for me every single recipe has its own story to tell, and has helped me to improve in some way – whether it's making a great nutritious mid-week dinner for the family, teaching Phoebe how to make cupcakes, or spilling loads of ingredients on the floor and having to start all over again (mistakes happen!). I have always liked recipes that are relatively simple and don't need ingredients that are too extravagant or expensive but can still taste great, and this book is full of these – the 7 Ways with Mince section (see pages 86 – 89) is a great example of this.

Each recipe contains a 'Barry Tip' plus a handy alternative to freshen things up, suggesting different ingredients or adjustments to suit that vegetarian sitting around the table, or if you need an excuse to make a dish again! . I want this book to be customisable for you to adapt, recipes like the Root Vegetable & Lentil Crowd-Pleaser (see page 159), Sea Bass and Prawn Kedgeree (see page 138) or the 'Thai Pad' (see page 47) are perfect places to start. I have also given each recipe a rating by eggs to reminisce from that first cooking experience (sniff).

🥚 – I feel that anyone could do these recipes
🥚🥚 – Slightly trickier steps involved
🥚🥚🥚 – Complex recipes that will require a good amount of concentration

I think I've rambled on enough now, so you can get cracking with some of these recipes. I absolutely love it when people make my recipes and share them with me on social media, so feel free to keep in touch via the links at the back of the book.

I have had loads of fun writing this book and hope you have fun cooking from it. Get the most from it, love it, stroke it like a cat and it will love you back! I hope you enjoy the book and fall in love with food in the way that I have – have fun and let everything from your supermarket, your butcher and your fruit and veg stall be your playground.

Laugh and learn folks, because if I can do it, absolutely ANYONE in the world can. Good luck!

Barry

A Few
BREKKY
IDEAS

⚡

BLACKBERRY PANCAKES
FRUIT & CRÈME FRAÎCHE BRIOCHE
EGGS BARRYDICT
BERRY & BANANA FRENCH TOAST
BUBBLE & SQUEAK POTATO BOATS
STRAWBERRY & BLUEBERRY GRANOLA
ALL-DAY BREAKFAST OMELETTE

Blackberry
PANCAKES

350g fresh blackberries (or drained from a tin if unable to forage!)

juice of ¼ lemon

150ml water

5 tbsp caster sugar

160g plain flour

1 tsp baking powder

pinch of salt

1 tbsp butter, plus extra for frying

160ml milk

1 large egg, beaten

½ tsp vanilla extract

To serve:

crème fraîche

This twist on American pancakes has a delicious blackberry and crème fraîche topping, which is a lot healthier than plastering them in chocolate sauce and golden syrup (which happens to be amazing too, FYI). These pancakes are light and foamy with a gentle vanilla taste and are super-easy to rustle up at any time of the day. Make these and I promise you'll wish you made a bigger batch.

1. Place all but a good handful of the blackberries in a saucepan over a medium heat with the lemon juice, 75ml of the water and 4 tablespoons of the sugar. Stir for a good 5 minutes until everything is combined.

2. Put the blackberry mix into a food processor and whizz until merged, adding more water until it reaches your desired consistency. It'll be thicker at first, but adding more water will thin it out – add and tweak with sugar and lemon if you like as well. Set aside.

3. Make the pancake batter by sifting the flour, baking powder, salt and remaining 1 tablespoon of sugar together into a bowl, then sift them all again. This will give the mix extra air. Melt the 1 tablespoon of butter in the microwave for 5 seconds and stir to loosen; you want it runny but cool – like Usain Bolt.

4. Pour the milk, egg, vanilla and cooled melted butter into the sifted flour and beat with a fork. Try to get rid of all the lumps, but it's not completely essential. Leave the batter to stand while you warm up a pan.

5. Heat a frying pan over a medium heat (use a griddle if you're feeling flash) and add a drop of butter. Once that starts to bubble, pour in a ladle-sized amount of batter and let it cook until you see bubbles regularly coming to the top of the pancake and popping, about 3 minutes. Flip over and cook for about 1–2 minutes until both sides are golden brown.

cont...

Barry's Tip

The pancake cooking times are a guide; they work well for me but keep your eye on them and top up the butter in the pan as needed to prevent burning.

Blackberry PANCAKES cont.

6. Make the pancakes in batches, topping up the butter in the pan as you go and stacking the cooked pancakes between greaseproof paper. You may want to do one pancake at a time depending on the size of your pan. You could add some squished blackberries to the batter to mix it up!

7. Serve with a good dollop of crème fraîche, a scattering of the reserved blackberries and the sauce drizzled over the top.

Why not try...

Putting spices into your pancake mix? You could add cinnamon or nutmeg to give it a lovely kick, especially if you serve them with some stewed apple too.

Fruit & Crème FRAÎCHE BRIOCHE

4 butter brioche (ideally round ones), halved

300ml low-fat crème fraîche, freshly chilled

zest and juice of ½ lime

acacia honey

butter, for spreading (optional)

1 mango, peeled and cut into chunks

2 kiwi fruit, peeled and cut into thin slices

handful of fresh strawberries, thinly sliced

chopped fresh mint (optional)

The cool thing about this colourful, fresh and fruity recipe is you can have it a couple of different ways; cold and soft (do nothing!), warm, and soft (microwave) or toasted (toaster or oven). Mrs Barry prefers hers toasted, Chloe likes it any way as long as it's in her mouth (she's not fussy), whereas Phoebe and I prefer it soft and a little more squidgy – cold and warm respectively. Whichever way you make it, enjoy this special fruity treat to give you a wicked start to the day.

1. If you want them toasted or warmed, prepare your brioche buns first. So whack them in a microwave on a short burst to soften quickly, in the oven on a tray with a bit of butter to toast (6–8 minutes), or even just the toaster (briefly) until you are happy – your choice. Of course you can just have them cold and slightly chewy, I'm not on commission, honest!

2. Combine the crème fraîche and lime zest and juice in a bowl, then add a little honey, say a teaspoon at first, but add more to your liking, and use a little more lime juice if you want.

3. Spread the brioche lightly with butter (if using, it's not essential), then smooth over a nice helping of the crème fraîche and sit the fruit randomly all over, grating over a little more lime, and sprinkling with mint to finish. Eat. Congratulations, you've just started your day with a bang, now go check your teeth for bits of mint – nobody wants to see that.

Why not try...

For those days when you need an added boost, use chocolate-chip brioche rolls or serve the rolls like mini fruit burgers, joining 2 halves. Yeah baby!

Barry's Tip

Have the fruit ready before mixing the crème fraîche, as you want it to be nice and refreshing. If the crème fraîche has sat at room temperature for too long it won't have the same punch.

knob of butter, plus extra for spreading

2 small gammon steaks

4 small mushrooms, finely chopped

2 egg yolks

1 tbsp lemon juice

pinch of salt

½ tsp cayenne pepper, to your liking

2 eggs

1 English muffin, cut in half

5 tbsp butter, melted in the microwave and almost bubbling hot

good handful of fresh curly leaf parsley, finely chopped

pepper

Barry's Tip
You don't have to use a pastry cutter on the gammon, although it does make it look super-cool.

I can't tell you how much I love this recipe – it's just stonkingly good; so, so good. First thing out of the way, we are making a sort of cheat's hollandaise sauce in a blender to save time, but it really does work. The textures and flavours that whirl through your mouth as you eat this will make you a very happy person indeed. Perfect for breakfast, lunch, dinner, midnight snack, last supper, etc.

1. Get a frying pan nice and hot over a medium heat, then plonk in a knob of butter and leave to melt. Once it starts to bubble, add the gammon steaks and cook for 6–8 minutes on each side until golden. Add the mushrooms for the last 5 minutes of cooking, to soften.

2. Whizz the egg yolks, lemon juice, salt and the cayenne pepper in a blender, then set aside.

3. Put a saucepan of water on to simmer, tip in the eggs and poach until the whites are set.

4. Toast the muffin halves until golden. Using a pastry cutter the same size as the muffins, cut the gammon into rounds, so it'll all look nice and funky. Dice the excess gammon for extra presentation or gobble up when no one is looking!

5. Gradually pour the 5 tablespoons of melted butter into the whisked egg yolks – whizz in batches of three until you are happy with the thickness, seasoning, adding extra cayenne or lemon juice as you like.

6. Serve by spreading a muffin half with a little butter, sitting the gammon on top, then the mushrooms, followed by a poached egg, a drizzle of hollandaise and a sprinkle of parsley and pepper.

Why not try...
Adding a couple of drops of Worcestershire or Tabasco sauce once it's served to give it a really lovely kick?

Eggs
BARRYDICT

Berry & Banana FRENCH TOAST

1 banana, peeled

40g raspberries

40g blueberries

1 tsp maple syrup, plus extra for dunking

2 slices white bread

1 egg

70ml milk

1 tsp ground cinnamon, plus extra for sprinkling (optional)

½ tsp vanilla essence

knob of butter

icing sugar, for dusting

To serve:

crispy bacon strips (optional)

Barry's Tip

Mixing the syrup with the fruit just takes a little sharpness off the raspberries; if you want a little more spank in yours, skip this step.

Oh where to start with this delicious breakfast? It's so naughty, but so right. I always thought French toast was something someone in France says when making a speech but, wow, if you don't already know what it is, get on board the ship, my friend! This is a banana, blueberry and raspberry version with good old maple syrup (you can use golden syrup if you prefer) – a truly scrumptious treat made in a hurry.

1. Mash together the banana and berries in a small bowl, then squirt on the teaspoon of maple syrup and mix together until combined.

2. Make the sandwich using the berry mixture as a filling and gently press down on the slices to hold them together.

3. Beat the egg, milk, cinnamon and vanilla together in a bowl until well combined. Dunk the sandwich in the mixture until coated. It should become a little heavier as it will absorb a lot of liquid like a sponge. Sprinkle some extra cinnamon on top of the bread if you are a big fan.

4. Melt the butter in a frying pan over a medium heat. Once melted and bubbling, add the coated sandwich and brown on both sides, about 3–4 minutes on each side. You can use a spatula to lift the sandwich up and check it's the colour you like before flipping.

5. Plonk the sandwich onto a plate lined with kitchen paper and dab to remove any excess grease. Dust the toasted sandwich lightly with icing sugar (you could put a little message in the bread, or dust a heart shape if you're feeling soppy) and serve with some extra maple syrup for dunking. It goes well with some crispy bacon strips, if you like.

Why not try...

Making peanut butter and jam sandwich versions of this – just as naughty!

Bubble & Squeak
POTATO BOATS

2 baking potatoes, washed and patted dry with kitchen paper

olive oil, for rubbing

salt and pepper

1 tbsp butter

½ small leek, thinly sliced

80g cabbage, finely chopped

2 tbsp light cream cheese

2 good handfuls of Cheddar cheese, grated

Barry's Tip
You can cook the potatoes to your liking. These are cooked longer to give a nice crispy outside to the potato – Mrs Barry often microwaves jacket potatoes in a hurry then finishes them off in the oven. My advice is to make these ahead in batches – it's worth the wait. Don't let Mrs Barry know that, though!

Mrs Barry is a good judge of jacket potatoes and in her words these twice-baked ones are 'amazing'. That's a pretty good compliment from the Buddha right there, and she's right; they just work brilliantly and are super-good. If you can time the baking of the potatoes, you can make these very quickly indeedy.

1. Preheat the oven to 190°C/170°C fan/375°F/Gas mark 5. Prick the potatoes with a fork a few times, then give them a lovely rub all over with olive oil (I find this strangely addictive) and sprinkle them with salt and pepper. Bake in the oven for a good 1½–2 hours until the skins are lovely and crisp. Allow to cool slightly.

2. Meanwhile, in a frying pan over a medium heat, melt the butter, then tip in the leek and cabbage and cook for about 10 minutes until softened and just before the vegetables start to brown.

3. When the potatoes are cool enough to handle, slice them in half, scoop out the potato flesh and put in a bowl.

4. Add the cream cheese, cabbage and leek to the potato flesh and mix well until fully incorporated. Season with salt and pepper, then pack the boats with their new passengers – throw the mixture in there, loading it up evenly. You can stack them pretty high, but don't go OTT – this isn't *Titanic* here, so you may have a little left over.

5. Top the boats with grated cheese and return to the oven to melt and brown the tops. Gobble immediately and send me a picture of your version.

Why not try...
Frying up some streaky bacon, then chopping it up and mixing it in with the cream cheese mixture?

Strawberry & BLUEBERRY GRANOLA

2 tsp acacia honey

2 tbsp good-quality vanilla yoghurt

handful of fresh strawberries, hulled and halved

handful of fresh blueberries

3 tbsp good-quality granola

Barry's Tip
This is very fast recipe, and if you don't want to present it nicely it can be even quicker – just throw all the ingredients into a bowl and eat!

Although this is a breakfast recipe – for which purpose it is amazing – granola can be eaten at any time of day. This recipe has a great combination of flavours and textures with a refreshing feel that can really kick-start your day – and the kids will love both building and eating this breakfast treat too.

1. Mix the honey with the yoghurt until well combined. Get a lovely-looking glass and spoon one-third of the honey yoghurt into the bottom. Add an even layer of strawberries, blueberries and granola, then top with yoghurt and repeat, finishing with a few strawberry and blueberry pieces on the top.

2. Eat straight away.

Why not try...
Putting this in plastic cups for your kids on the school run or take the ingredients to work in plastic tubs, then prepare them super-speedily for a midday energy kick?

All-day BREAKFAST OMELETTE

Difficulty ●
Ready in 20 MINUTES
Serves 1

2 good-quality sausages

salt and pepper

1 tbsp olive oil, plus 1 tsp

4 cherry tomatoes, halved

½ yellow pepper, deseeded and diced

4 button mushrooms, halved

1 spring onion, sliced

3 eggs

1 tbsp grated Cheddar cheese, plus extra for topping (optional)

handful of fresh parsley, chopped, plus extra for sprinkling (optional)

knob of butter

I love this speedy omelette as you can do so many different things to it. The cool thing about this one is that it's a relatively basic omelette base with a little cheese and herbs, which has some cheeky extras folded in. You can really make it your own – lose the sausages and it's vegetarian. Ramp it up with different herb combos or added spice and love it! Great any time of day.

1. Using your fingertips, squeeze out small balls from the sausages, discarding the skins. You should get 3–4 per sausage. Halve the balls and season with a little salt and pepper.

2. In a frying pan over a medium heat, add the 1 tablespoon of olive oil, then cook the sausage balls for 2–3 minutes until lightly coloured. Add the tomatoes, pepper, mushrooms and spring onions and cook until the vegetables are softened and the sausage balls are browned all over. Remove from the pan.

3. Using a fork, lightly beat the eggs, then add the Cheddar and parsley and season with salt and pepper. Gently mix again to combine. This is the omelette mixture done.

4. When ready to make the omelette, warm the frying pan over a medium heat, add the remaining 1 teaspoon of oil and the butter and leave to melt. Once it starts to bubble, gently pour in the omelette mixture, tilting the pan so the omelette covers the base evenly, and gently pushing any large puddles of egg sat on top out to the sides with a spatula.

5. Cook until golden brown on one side, about 90 seconds, then lift the edge with the spatula to check. Lift the omelette out and flip over to brown the other side, about a minute. Place the omelette on a plate and spoon in the cooked vegetables and sausages in a strip down the centre of the omelette, season it and top with extra cheese, if you wish. Fold up and enjoy.

Why not try...

Making an Indian omelette? My friend Bini did a video with me making one; just adding a few awesome spices to the egg mixture can drastically change the final taste.

Barry's Tip

Be careful when cooking the sausages; keep the ball sizes consistent and make sure they are properly cooked through, not just browned on the outside!

POULTRY

CHICKEN & BACON CAESAR SALAD
PIRI PIRI CHICKEN WINGS
CHICKEN SATAY CURRY
GERT LUSH DRUNK CHICKEN PIE
JERK CHICKEN LEGS
SHREDDED SWEET CHILLI CHICKEN FAJITAS
TRAFFIC-LIGHT THAI CHICKEN CURRY
ROAST CHICKEN WITH LEMON HERB BUTTER
CORNFLAKE CHICKEN DIPPERS WITH A HONEY MUSTARD DIP
CHICKEN THIGH & HALLOUMI TRAYBAKE
CHICKEN TIKKA PITTAS
'THAI PAD'
CHICKEN EN PAPILLOTE
ASIAN CHICKEN BROTH
GRIDDLED TURKEY TWISTER LOLLIES
CAULIFLOWER BASE BBQ CHICKEN PIZZA
CHICKEN, AUBERGINE & APRICOT TAGINE
SPATCHCOCK CHICKEN PARMESAN
KOREAN COLA CHICKEN

Chicken & Bacon
CAESAR SALAD

2 chicken breasts, cut into slithers

salt and pepper

2 tbsp mayonnaise

3 anchovy fillets

40g grated Parmesan, plus extra for shavings

drop of Worcestershire sauce

zest of ½ lemon

4 bacon rashers, cut into strips

knob of butter

2 slices white day-old bread ideally, crusts removed and cut into cubes

1 tbsp olive oil

2 baby gem lettuces, chopped

Barry's Tip

Keep your eye on the croutons as you make them, because they won't take that long and can burn quickly in a hot pan. Flip them with care.

I love a good Caesar salad – that great combination of cheese and crunchy salad. Here I've added the classic chicken and bacon combo to my homemade dressing and crunchy croutons. It's fast, delicious and the sort of dish where you want to learn to moonwalk after eating it – hee hee, shamone, etc.

1. Season the chicken with a little salt and pepper and set aside.

2. Make the dressing by blending the mayo, anchovies, Parmesan, Worcestershire sauce and lemon zest together until combined. Season to taste and tweak to your liking. If you want to thin the sauce out a little, gradually add some water and blend again.

3. Meanwhile, cook the bacon in a frying pan over a medium heat for a good 10–15 minutes until crispy. Keep turning the bacon until it has firmed up and dried a little, then put on a plate and set aside.

4. Heat a smaller frying pan over a medium heat and add the butter. Once melted, throw in the bread cubes and fry, turning them over for 3–4 minutes until lightly golden. Put on a plate lined with kitchen paper and sprinkle over a little salt and pepper.

5. When the bacon is done, add the olive oil to the pan and fry the chicken for about 3–4 minutes until lightly browned. Take a piece out to check that it's cooked through.

6. To serve, toss the lettuce pieces with some Parmesan shavings, most of the chicken, the bacon (which you can snap into smaller pieces if you wish) and the croutons. Drizzle over the dressing, then top with the remaining bacon, chicken and croutons, and finish with a good seasoning of salt and pepper.

Why not try...

Filling out the salad further with cherry tomatoes and avocado or grilling the chicken and bacon instead of frying them?

Piri Piri CHICKEN WINGS

While writing this recipe I experienced my first Nandos; the piri piri plate is hugely popular and some Bristol Rugby players often tweet about visits there. My mates dragged me along and I enjoyed it, but really there's nothing better than making your own. This recipe uses chicken wings drenched in a yummy homemade piri piri sauce that you can tweak any way you like.

1 medium red chilli, cut in half and deseeded

2 garlic cloves, peeled

3 lemons

1 tsp smoked paprika

1 tsp ground ginger

1 tsp caster sugar

½ tsp salt

12 chicken wings

olive oil, for brushing

3 tbsp butter, melted

handful of chopped fresh coriander, plus extra for sprinkling (optional)

To serve:

Rainbow Coleslaw (see page 220)

potato wedges

1. Whizz the chilli, garlic, juice of 2 lemons, paprika, ginger, sugar and salt together in a food processor until well combined. Taste to make sure you're happy. You can push the chilli quantities for extreme hotness, if you like!

2. Rinse the chicken wings and pat dry with kitchen paper, then place them in something that will fit in your fridge – with limited space in our fridge a freezer bag works best. Pour the marinade around the wings, massage briefly, then close the bag or cover and leave to marinate for at least 1 hour.

3. Once ready to cook, preheat the oven to 220°C/200°C fan/425°F/ Gas mark 7 and brush a lined baking tray with olive oil. Put the chicken on the tray (keeping any leftover marinade), then if you have a lemon half lying about rub that on the chicken. Bake in the oven for about 25–30 minutes. Pour out any oil and top up with the leftover marinade, leaving about 1½ tablespoons for later. Decrease the oven temperature to 200°C/180°C fan/400°F/Gas mark 6 and cook for another 20 minutes, flipping the chicken pieces over a few times, until there's a lovely colour on the outside and they are cooked through. Keep your eye on them. Remove from the oven and leave to rest.

4. Meanwhile, mix the leftover marinade, melted butter, chopped coriander and 1 tablespoon of lemon juice together. Using a pastry brush, brush a light coating of the mixture over the chicken, then sprinkle with more coriander, if you like. Serve with Rainbow Coleslaw and potato wedges.

Why not try...

Using other pieces of chicken – marinate in exactly the same way, but adjust the cooking times to suit the particular cut of chicken? Or use prawns or strips of steak on the BBQ?

Chicken
SATAY
CURRY

1 tbsp olive oil

500g chicken breast, cut into large cubes

salt and pepper

1 garlic clove, finely chopped

1 red pepper, deseeded and diced

1 tbsp Thai red curry paste

2 tbsp smooth peanut butter

1 tbsp mango chutney

400ml tin coconut milk

1 lemongrass stalk, fat end bashed

handful unsalted peanuts, bashed, plus extra to garnish

100ml vegetable stock

zest and juice of 1 lime, plus 4 wedges to serve

handful chopped fresh coriander

200g mangetout

To serve:

rice

I love this; I think possibly due to a growing obsession with peanut butter, but nonetheless if you are after a no-fuss speedy dinner with a little kick, look no further! I use a little Thai red curry paste to give this some heat, and you can add more, but there's just a nice nutty vibe going through this dish that I find very addictive.

1. Put the oil into a pan over a medium heat and cook the chicken until sealed all over. Season with a little pepper, if you wish, then add the garlic and red pepper and cook for a further 1–2 minutes before plonking in the Thai paste and mixing well to coat all over. Warm this for another minute or so.

2. Add the peanut butter, mango chutney, coconut milk, lemongrass, peanuts, vegetable stock, lime zest and juice and most of the coriander and season with salt and pepper. Warm through on a low simmer for 15 minutes. Add the mangetout and cook for a further 5 minutes, then take out the lemongrass and make any final taste tweaks – adding seasoning or extra lime, etc.

3. Serve with some extra bashed peanuts on top, more coriander, lime wedges and rice of your choice.

Why not try...

Making your own Thai red curry paste to go with this recipe? It will take a little longer but that way you can really customise it, using some of the ingredients already used above in whatever strength you like.

Barry's Tip
Increase the amount of curry paste used or add a freshly chopped red chilli if you want a little more punch. Swap the chicken for lean diced pork, if you like.

Gert Lush DRUNK CHICKEN PIE

1 tbsp olive oil

400g skinless and boneless chicken breast or thighs, cut into chunks

1 leek (roughly 200g), trimmed and sliced

60g unsalted butter

2 heaped tbsp plain flour, plus extra for dusting

300ml full-fat milk, plus extra for brushing

200ml cider, such as Thatchers

pepper

170g broccoli, cut into small florets

handful of chopped fresh parsley

198g tin sweetcorn, drained

320g pack ready-rolled puff pastry sheet

Barry's Tip
Don't be alarmed with how thick the roux gets when you initially add the liquid; keep stirring and add it slowly and it'll be sweet.

'Gert Lush', according to the urban dictionary, is the highest form of praise to be given to anything by a Bristolian. Well, that's what's going on right here in this delicious no-fuss chicken pie. A combination of sweetcorn, broccoli, leeks and a good drop of decent cider bubbling away creates something awesome. Give this one a try!

1. Preheat the oven to 200°C/180°C fan/400°F/Gas mark 6.

2. Heat a frying pan over a medium heat, add the olive oil and chicken and cook until the meat is sealed all over. Add the leek and cook for 5–6 minutes more, stirring every now and then until it has softened and the chicken is starting to brown. Turn off the heat and set aside.

3. Now make the roux (cool name, huh?). Melt the butter in a separate saucepan over a low heat. Add the flour and cook, stirring as it thickens to avoid any lumps, for 2 minutes. Slowly add the milk and cider, a little at a time, mixing the liquid in fully and working out any lumps before adding any more. Once fully mixed, season with pepper and simmer for 3–4 minutes until thick.

4. Tip the sauce, broccoli, parsley and sweetcorn into the chicken pan, stir well, then simmer gently for a further 5 minutes. Season the sauce with a good grind of pepper, then set aside to cool slightly.

5. On a floured work surface, unroll the pastry and cut out a lid 2cm larger than your 1-litre pie dish to allow for any shrinkage.

6. When ready to make the pie, pour the slightly cooled mixture into the dish and top with your pastry lid. Cut off any excess that's hanging over the edge and use a fork to press the pastry to the side of the dish. Make a few slits in the top of the pie to let the steam escape, then brush the top with a little milk and bake in the oven for a good 25–30 minutes until golden brown and puffed up.

Why not try...
You will have some excess pastry, so why not get creative with some funky shapes or spell out a secret message – no marriage proposals on a pie though, please!

Jerk CHICKEN LEGS

6 chicken legs (with thighs attached)

1 tbsp olive oil, for frying

For the marinade:

1½ Scotch bonnet peppers, deseeded

1 tbsp allspice

pinch of ground cinnamon

pinch of ground nutmeg

½ red onion, peeled and chopped

2 spring onions, trimmed and chopped

1 tbsp lemon thyme leaves

2cm piece of fresh ginger, peeled and chopped

1 tbsp olive oil

1 garlic clove, peeled and chopped

2 tbsp light soy sauce

pinch of salt

2 tsp light brown sugar

zest and juice of 1 lemon

To serve:

sweet potato wedges
(see page 223)

Avocado Salsa
(see page 220)

The combo of spices used in this dish go a little against what I stand for – I like to keep things super-easy – but this is really simple, and once you've made it you will agree with me. Of course, you can get ready-made jerk flavouring, but there's nothing better than making it yourself to control the heat. Here the chicken legs are drenched in a great jerk marinade, scorched up a bit, then oven cooked until they're jammin! (Bad Jamaican reference...)

1. Whizz all the ingredients for the marinade together in a food processor until well combined. It may need a final stir with a spoon. Taste and adjust the flavour – if you want it hotter add another chilli (or keep the seeds in), if sweeter then add more sugar, if spicier add more allspice, etc.

2. Using a knife, score the chicken legs quite deeply, then put them in a freezer bag. Add the marinade and work it in with your fingers and thumbs (scene from *Ghost*). Close the bag and refrigerate, ideally overnight but at least for a few hours.

3. When you're ready to cook the chicken, preheat the oven to 190°C/170°C fan/375°F/Gas mark 5. Heat the olive oil in a frying pan, then add the chicken, pressing down on the legs and cooking until there is a lovely colour on both sides – try to get a lightly darkened BBQ effect.

4. Put the legs into an ovenproof tray, cover and bake in the oven for 50 minutes or until cooked through. Check halfway through, draining off any excess juices and topping up with any of the leftover marinade, if necessary. Serve with some pan juices spooned over the legs. It's great with some sweet potato wedges and Avocado Salsa.

Why not try...

Spreading this marinade over some fish on the BBQ and cooking on either side with a squeeze of lemon juice? I'd imagine you'd be pretty darn close to heaven right there.

Shredded
SWEET CHILLI
CHICKEN
FAJITAS

2 chicken breasts

salt and pepper

1 tbsp olive oil

1 onion, peeled and diced

1 red pepper, deseeded and cut into thin strips

1 courgette, thinly sliced

2 mushrooms, sliced

390g carton or 400g tin chopped tomatoes

2 tsp smoked paprika

4 tbsp sweet chilli sauce, plus extra to serve (optional)

4 tortillas

4 tbsp crème fraîche

small handful of fresh chives, chopped

100g Red Leicester cheese, grated

To serve:

rice and/or salad

Barry's Tip
If you want it hotter, wrap in foil and place in a preheated oven for a couple of minutes.

You'll see in this book that I like using tortillas – I've found them super-good to make filling, cheap, tasty midweek dinners in a hurry, and this one is no exception. Here I've poached and shredded a chicken and served it in an ingredient-packed wrap with a tangy sauce and cheese and crème fraîche layers. This is a personal favourite of mine, which you can tweak away once you've made it a few times.

1. Drop the chicken breasts into a saucepan of lightly salted simmering water. Keep over a low simmer and poach for 12 minutes. Turn off the heat, cover with a lid and leave to stand for a further 10 minutes while you crack on with the rest of the dish.

2. Heat the olive oil in a frying pan over a medium heat, then add the onion and cook for a good 4–5 minutes to soften. Add the red pepper, courgette and mushrooms and cook for another 5 minutes.

3. Add the tomatoes and a teaspoon of paprika, mix to combine, then bring to a simmer and cook until it has reduced down. When the mixture is slightly thickened, add the sweet chilli sauce and mix to combine. This will also thicken and caramelise the sauce slightly.

4. Remove the chicken to a chopping board and, using 2 forks, shred it into pieces. Once shredded, put it in a bowl and add the remaining paprika and season with a little black pepper. Mix until the chicken is lightly coated, then tweak the flavourings to taste.

5. Warm the tortillas in the microwave for 10 seconds, then put a strip of the tomato chilli mixture along the length of each tortilla, adding a good handful of shredded chicken on top. Spread some crème fraîche, chives and grated cheese on top of that, then roll up and serve with a side salad and/or rice and more sweet chilli sauce, if you like.

Why not try...
Packing the wraps with rice, rolling up and taking one to work for a very special lunch?

Traffic-Light
THAI CHICKEN
CURRY

1 tbsp olive oil

700g chicken breasts

2 lemongrass stalks, outer leaves removed

5 green chillies, deseeded and roughly chopped

3 garlic cloves, peeled and halved

4cm piece of fresh ginger, peeled

1½ tsp ground cumin

1 tbsp fish sauce, plus extra to flavour

40g fresh coriander stalks

1 green pepper, deseeded and cut into small squares

1 red pepper, deseeded and cut into small squares

1 yellow pepper, deseeded and cut into small squares

6 kaffir lime leaves

400ml coconut milk

¼ pint chicken stock

salt and pepper

chopped fresh coriander, to garnish

To serve:

rice

Okay, first things first, there are no traffic lights in this curry, but it is a pretty stonking green curry indeed. I have made similar dishes before with shop-bought curry paste, which tastes good, but this is so much better. I really hope you try this one, as it's a beautiful-tasting dish.

1. Heat the oil over a medium heat, then add the chicken breasts and brown on both sides. Once done, slice the chicken into small cubes.

2. Meanwhile, whizz the lemongrass, chillies, garlic, ginger, cumin, fish sauce and coriander stalks together in a blender or food processor until combined, then set aside.

3. Add the peppers to the pan, still over a medium heat, and fry until they just start to char around the edges. Add your whizzed mixture and stir for 1–2 minutes until the peppers are coated.

4. Load up the pan with the chicken pieces, kaffir lime leaves, coconut milk and stock, stirring well to combine. Simmer for 15 minutes to reduce the sauce slightly and to allow the chicken to cook through. Season to taste with a little extra fish sauce, and salt and pepper. Garnish with chopped coriander and serve with rice of your choice.

Why not try...

Using some of the leftover chicken from the Roast Chicken with Lemon Herb Butter on page 41? This will save you cooking the chicken, just chuck it in at the end, coat and warm through.

Barry's Tip
If you don't want to make the homemade green paste, use some good-quality shop-bought paste instead.

Roast Chicken with
LEMON HERB BUTTER

100g unsalted butter, softened

5 fresh sage leaves, finely chopped

handful of fresh parsley, finely chopped

4 fresh thyme sprigs, leaves picked, chopped

5 garlic cloves, peeled and 1 clove crushed

zest of 1 lemon, then cut into small wedges

salt and pepper

1.4kg whole free-range chicken, string removed

olive oil, for rubbing, plus extra for coating

1 red onion, peeled and cut into small wedges

handful of baby potatoes, cut in half

1 parsnip, peeled and cut into small chunks

2 carrots, peeled and thinly sliced

Barry's Tip
Make sure that all your veg chunks are of equal size, otherwise they will not cook through at the same rate. Use a large-enough roasting tin to accommodate the chicken and the vegetables.

This is a bit of a 'go-to' recipe for you to use and play around with. The great thing about this dish is it's relatively subtle in flavour but has a slight lemon vibe passing through it. As the chicken is cooked in a tray of vegetables it's pretty much dinner in a tray, and, hey, if you have any leftover chicken, there's plenty of other recipes in this book you can use it in.

1. Preheat the oven to 200°C/180°C fan/400°F/Gas mark 6.

2. Mix the butter, sage, parsley, thyme, the crushed garlic clove and the lemon zest together until fully combined. Season with a little salt and pepper.

3. Loosen the skin on the breast and thighs of the chicken with your fingers and push the herby butter mixture into the gap so that it's trapped between the meat and skin. Rub olive oil over the top of the chicken and grind over a little pepper.

4. Sit the chicken, breast-side up, in a large roasting tin and scatter the lemon and onion wedges around the chicken.

5. Meanwhile, mix the potatoes, parsnip, carrots, the whole garlic cloves and a small drop of olive oil together in a bowl until the vegetables are lightly coated in the oil. Season and then spread the vegetables all around the edge of the roasting tin, preferably in a single layer.

6. Roast the chicken in the oven for 1 hour–1 hour 20 minutes or until the juices of the chicken run clear when a skewer is inserted into the thigh. Keep your eye on the way your chicken is browning – you may want to turn the tin round to make sure it's browning evenly.

7. Once ready, let the chicken rest for 15 minutes before carving and serving with the roasted vegetables.

Why not try...
Spatchcocking the chicken like in the Spatchcock Chicken Parmesan recipe on page 59 and cooking the bottom of the chicken in the oven, and flipping it over halfway through?

Cornflake Chicken Dippers
WITH A HONEY MUSTARD DIP

2 chicken breasts (about 450g)

90g cornflakes

¼ tsp paprika (optional)

pepper

1 large egg, beaten

3 tsp runny honey

3 tsp Dijon mustard

2 heaped tbsp low-fat mayonnaise

It would be wrong for me to deny that I've tasted breaded chicken from a well-known pizza chain in the past, but here's a really cool way to make some delicious cornflake (yes, cornflake) chicken strips that you can tweak to your liking and serve with a lovely honey mustard dip for dunking.

1. Preheat the oven to 220°C/200°C fan/425°F/Gas mark 7 and line a baking tray with greaseproof paper.

2. Slice the chicken in half lengthways, then cut into strips.

3. Put the cornflakes into a freezer bag, seal and lightly bash with a rolling pin until they are small – this is quite a fun task! Pour the paprika, if using, and ½ teaspoon of pepper into the freezer bag with the cornflakes, seal and shake to combine (dancing is optional).

4. Combine the beaten egg with 2 teaspoons each of honey and mustard, stirring gently.

5. Have the egg mixture, cornflakes and baking tray laid out in that order. Coat the chicken all over in the egg mixture, then drop them into the cornflake bag and shake until well coated. Sit the coated chicken carefully on the baking tray and repeat for all the remaining chicken. If there are any gaps in the cornflake coating, pat some on with your fingers. Bake on the middle shelf in the oven, turning halfway through, for 12 minutes until golden brown and cooked through – cut a piece in half to make sure.

6. Meanwhile, to make the honey mustard dip, simply mix the mayo, remaining teaspoon each of mustard and honey together in a small bowl and pour into a dipping pot. Season with black pepper, tweak to taste and chill until needed.

7. When the chicken is golden brown, serve with the honey mustard dip. You can make the dish into a main course by serving with some rustic mashed potato and minty peas.

Why not try...
Getting children to try these? Cut into small pieces as healthier nuggets, let them dunk them in ketchup instead and only tell them afterwards that it's cornflakes. The girls love these.

Barry's Tip
Don't worry about the cornflake smell when you are dipping into the egg; after baking this goes away, honest!

Chicken Thigh & HALLOUMI TRAYBAKE

green, red and yellow peppers, deseeded and sliced into squares

1 red onion, peeled and cut into wedges

handful of new potatoes, cut in half

1 tbsp olive oil

1 tsp pepper

2 tsp dried basil

450g chicken thigh fillets

200g halloumi cheese, sliced

handful of black olives, pitted and thinly sliced

handful of fresh basil leaves

Barry's Tip
If you can't grill the chicken after adding the halloumi, then simply return the dish to the oven to brown.

In this recipe delicious chicken thighs are baked with vegetables, then topped with a sprinkling of halloumi, olives and fresh basil. These flavours work really well together, and with a slight salty edge it works a charm. What's even better is that it's all cooked in one tray – easy peasy!

1. Preheat the oven to 180°C/160°C fan/350°F/Gas mark 4.

2. Mix the vegetables with most of the olive oil, pepper and half the dried basil in a bowl until all the vegetables are coated.

3. Arrange the chicken thighs in a tray, then brush with a little oil and sprinkle with the remaining dried basil. Scatter the vegetables around the chicken and bake in the oven for about 25 minutes or until the thighs are cooked through. Check by making a little cut through a couple of thighs to be sure. If the meat is pink, bake a little longer.

4. Preheat the grill to Medium. When the chicken is cooked, top with the halloumi and black olives and grill until the cheese is golden and melting. Serve the chicken sprinkled with basil leaves and with the vegetables on the side.

Why not try...
Scattering some cubes of pancetta into the roasting dish or wrapping the chicken in bacon before baking?

Chicken Tikka PITTAS

1 tsp paprika

2.5cm piece of fresh ginger, peeled

3 garlic cloves, peeled and chopped

1 tbsp garam masala

3 tsp ground cumin

1 tsp chilli powder

juice of 1 lemon

125g natural yoghurt, plus extra to serve

2 skinless chicken breasts, cut into small chunks

4 pittas

To serve:

lettuce

tomato

mango chutney

lemon wedges

chopped fresh coriander

Deliciously simple marinated chicken tikka pittas right here! Marinating chunks of chicken in a homemade yoghurt marinade really creates a taste sensation. Straight from the grill these pittas are moist and juicy, doubled up with the crunch of vegetables and tangy mango chutney. You'll love them...I hope!

1. Make the marinade by whizzing the paprika, ginger, garlic, garam masala, cumin, chilli powder, lemon juice and the yoghurt together in a food processor until well combined. Alternatively, grate the garlic and ginger, then mix all the ingredients together with a wooden spoon. Tweak this marinade to your liking, if you wish.

2. Put the yoghurt marinade in a sealable bag, then drop in the chicken and massage it until it is coated. Seal and whack in the fridge for at least 2 hours, but preferably overnight. You can even do this before you leave for work in the morning.

3. When you're ready to cook, preheat the grill to Medium. Put the chicken under the grill and cook, turning until golden brown all over and cooked through. I gave mine a good 15 minutes, but cut through a chunk of chicken to make sure it's cooked before removing.

4. Toast the pittas and stuff them with the chicken pieces, lettuce, tomato, chutney, a squirt of lemon juice and some chopped coriander on top. If you have any leftover yoghurt you can chuck this in too.

Why not try...
Serving alongside some basmati rice for a more filling alternative or BBQ the chicken, weather permitting?

Barry's Tip
Don't worry if there is a slight burning when cooking the chicken under the grill; a little marinade will do that, but it's far cleaner than using a frying pan.

Thai Pad

400g boneless chicken thighs, chopped into chunks

2 tbsp soy sauce

2.5cm piece of fresh ginger, finely chopped

200g rice noodles, Thai if you can get them

3 limes, 1 cut into wedges

2 tbsp fish sauce

1 tbsp sweet chilli sauce

2 tbsp brown sugar

salt and pepper

2 tbsp sesame oil

1 red chilli, deseeded and chopped

2 shallots, finely sliced

4 cloves garlic, crushed

60ml chicken stock

50g beansprouts

good handful fresh coriander, chopped

2 spring onions, sliced

40g cashews, roughly chopped

This delicious street-food-style stir-fry was first introduced to me by my mate Ali Mills, who was lucky enough to spend some time in Thailand – he rates this as one of the best things he tried out there (other than eating a live scorpion, apparently!). This is a chicken version, with a nice kick and a good helping of noodles alongside. I know this is the second Thai chicken dish in the book, but it's so different and so worth it!

1. Marinate the chicken pieces in a bowl of soy sauce with the ginger. Set aside.

2. Meanwhile, cook the noodles for 4–5 minutes in a saucepan of simmering water, drain, refresh under cold running water, then return to the pan and top it up with cold water to keep them loose.

3. In a bowl, combine the juice of 2 limes and a little zest, fish sauce, sweet chilli sauce, brown sugar and a pinch of pepper and leave to one side. It should be a nice balance of lime, but tweak it to your liking.

4. Have all the other ingredients ready. Warm the sesame oil in a wok over a medium heat, drop in the red chilli, shallots and garlic and fry for a minute. Add the chicken, pouring in the marinade and stock a little at a time (it's best not to have it too wet) and fry until the chicken is completely cooked through. Take out a piece of chicken and cut through with a knife to make sure it's cooked before moving forward.

5. Next, chuck the rest in – the beansprouts, drained noodles, the zingy fish sauce mixture, half the coriander, spring onions and cashews, cooking for a good 2–3 minutes until completely coated and well mixed – it should be smelling really good now, so make any final tweaks you wish, but work quickly!

6. Serve with the remaining coriander, spring onions and cashews sprinkled over the top with some more sweet chilli sauce and lime wedges alongside.

Why not try...
Mixing it up to make a vegetarian version with some of your favourite veggies, or create a fishy vibe using king prawns?

Chicken
EN PAPILLOTE

2 medium chicken breasts, kept whole or sliced into chunks diagonally

100g asparagus tips, halved lengthways

10 baby potatoes, thinly sliced

1 tbsp olive oil

small handful of fresh lemon thyme leaves

zest of 1 lemon

1 garlic clove, peeled and finely chopped

salt and pepper

handful of spinach leaves

To serve:

your favourite vegetables

Barry's Tip

Make sure your parcel is completely sealed, and sit it seam-side down on the baking tray to make sure everything stays in the package.

Cooking *en papillote* is French for 'in parchment' (although you can use foil but 'chicken *en papier d'aluminium*' doesn't sound as cool!) – essentially to cook inside a parcel. This is a great way of cooking both savoury and sweet foods and helps to keep all the flavour locked in while steaming the food. Here the chicken is sealed in a pouch with asparagus, lemon and thyme vibes – such a simple thing to try, hope you give it a go!

1. Preheat the oven to 180°C/160°C fan/350°F/ Gas mark 4. Cut out 2 pieces of baking parchment into 40 x 40cm squares, each big enough to comfortably wrap the chicken.

2. Put the chicken, asparagus and potatoes into a bowl and cover with the olive oil, thyme, lemon zest, garlic and plenty of seasoning. Get your hands into the bowl and mix together.

3. Put the ingredients to one side of the parchment (make this look as pretty as you like), adding the spinach too, then fold the parchment over, and crimp and fold the edges all the way round so it looks a bit like a Cornish pasty.

4. Put the chicken parcels on a baking tray and cook for 20 minutes. Check one parcel by making a little incision to make sure that the chicken is cooked through. Serve on a plate with some of the juices from the parcel drizzled over. It goes great with more vegetables.

Why not try...

Fish *en papillote* is extremely popular and can help to flavour the fish, so try the same idea and make a sweet version of bananas with chocolate chips. This is a great treat for kids – play around with it.

2 skinless chicken breasts or thighs, cut into thin strips

1.2 litres chicken stock

1 baby bok choy, sliced

80g mangetout, snipped at angles

4 spring onions, sliced into small sections at angles

1 fresh red chilli, deseeded and sliced into thin strips

1 garlic clove, peeled and finely chopped

4 shiitake mushrooms, quartered

juice of 1 lime

1 tsp fish sauce, or to taste

1 tsp soy sauce, or to taste

salt and pepper

chopped fresh coriander, for sprinkling

Whoo, this soupy broth will get you going! It's got a kick, but just enough, and just like the main ingredient used here (chicken), you can switch it up any way you want and make it as naughty as you like. For such a quick rustle-together bowl, there's a lot of love in there.

1. In a saucepan, poach the chicken in the stock over a medium heat for about 6–8 minutes until cooked through.

2. Throw in the bok choy, mangetout, spring onions, chilli, garlic and mushrooms and simmer for at least 5 minutes to soften.

3. Squirt in half the lime juice, the fish and soy sauces and salt and pepper, then stir, adding more sauces and seasoning to taste until you are happy with the flavour. Serve with chopped coriander sprinkled over the top.

Why not try...

I have gone for a chicken broth here, but there's nothing stopping you keeping it veggie or adding other meats or even perhaps making it a funky prawn broth – all good, baby!

Barry's Tip
Adding some of this broth alongside freshly cooked noodles will transform the dish from a speedy filler into a hearty dinner.

Griddled TURKEY TWISTER LOLLIES

Difficulty ●●
Ready in **30 MINUTES**
Serves 2–3

60g cranberry sauce

60ml white wine vinegar

60g caster sugar

1 tbsp soy sauce

3 turkey fillets, roughly about 260g

salt and pepper

zest and juice of 1 lemon

5 fresh sage leaves, chopped

olive oil, for brushing

Barry's Tip

It's important to keep the lollies thin on the sticks. If you make them too big they will look grossly out of proportion (and a bit scary!), but most importantly they will take a lot longer to cook through – and nobody likes medium-rare turkey!

This is my sort of recipe dedication to Jamie Oliver. He campaigned against 'turkey twizzlers', a sort of processed turkey meat thing on a stick being fed to kids in schools – I remember actually seeing them myself when I was at school too! This recipe makes a delicious, zingy homemade version that kids of all ages will love, and despite the turkey/cranberry reference, it's not just for Santa and can be eaten all year round!

1. For the cranberry sauce dip, mix the cranberry sauce, vinegar, sugar and soy sauce together in a saucepan and stir over a medium heat until simmering and combined. Lower the heat and let bubble lightly for 10 minutes. Check the flavour and tweak how you like it; this is quite sweet and zingy so you may want to add more soy sauce or reduce the amount of vinegar. Remove from the heat, pour into a jug and allow to cool.

2. Preheat the oven to 200°C/180°C fan/400°F/Gas mark 6. Put a sheet of greaseproof paper on a chopping board, place a turkey fillet on top, then put another sheet of greaseproof paper over and bash the fillet with your rolling pin until it is evenly thin all over. Don't get over-excited with the bashing as you don't want to split the turkey.

3. Once all the fillets are flattened, season them with a good pinch of salt and pepper, then sprinkle the lemon zest and sage leaves evenly between them. Squeeze a little squirt of lemon juice on each one – literally ¼ teaspoon per fillet. Press the toppings slightly with your fingers, then slice your turkey rectangle into three sections lengthways.

4. Thread one end of the turkey section through a skewer, rotating as you go to create a spiral effect. Repeat with all the turkey pieces. It should look like a spring!

5. Heat a griddle pan until hot, brush the lollies with olive oil, then griddle until golden brown all over and cooked through.

cont...

6. To make sure the turkey is cooked, put the twisters on a baking tray and bake on the middle shelf in the oven for about 6 minutes to cook through. Once done, using a pastry brush, brush each of the lollies with a light coating of the cranberry sauce mixture. Phoebe likes to use the leftover sauce as a dipping pot as it increases the sweetness of the turkey!

Why not try...

If you are making these twisters for a child you may find that they aren't keen on sage, so swap it with some freshly chopped parsley or coriander instead. You could even mix it up with different types of fillings, perhaps making different ones with orange, lemon and lime zest and a small squidge of citrus juice, then have a guessing game of 'What's in the lolly?'.

Cauliflower Base
BBQ CHICKEN PIZZA

oil, for oiling

400g cauliflower head (no stalk please)

1 large egg, beaten

100g grated mozzarella cheese

½ tsp onion powder

½ tsp garlic powder

1 tsp dried mixed herbs

1 tsp paprika

Topping:

2 tbsp barbecue sauce

small handful of cooked chicken breast slices

1 tbsp tinned sweetcorn, drained

1 mushroom, peeled and sliced

small handful of uncooked bacon rashers, cut into chunks

good handful of grated mozzarella cheese, for sprinkling

This is something that I have fallen in love with along my journey; such a simple concept and one that I'd never thought possible before – replacing the doughy base of a pizza with one made from a vegetable! Combine this with one of my most favourite pizza toppings (BBQ chicken) and you've got this little beauty.

1. Preheat the oven to 200°C/180°C fan/400°F/Gas mark 6. Grate the cauliflower into pieces until you are left with a pile that looks like flaky polystyrene.

2. Put the cauliflower into a bowl, it'll be slightly moist, then microwave, uncovered, for 9 minutes. (I have an 800-watt microwave, so if yours is slightly higher it may take a little less time.) Your kitchen may start to smell of cauliflower as it breaks down, but don't worry, that's all good.

3. Once the cauliflower has softened slightly, give it a stir and pour the egg, mozzarella cheese, onion and garlic powders, herbs and paprika into a bowl. Mix it with a wooden spoon until it forms a sort of putty mixture – the egg and cheese are holding that baby all together.

4. Place the mixture onto a greased baking tray and use your hands to push out and form your base shape – make sure it's even all the way around and try to get it about half an inch thick.

5. Bake for 8–10 minutes until lightly golden brown, the cheese may bubble slightly. Prepare your toppings while it's in the oven.

6. Once done, remove from the oven and leave to cool. For the BBQ pizza I spread on 2 tablespoons barbecue sauce – make sure you cover the whole base as you don't want it to burn. Top with the cooked chicken, sweetcorn, mushroom, uncooked bacon chunks and a further sprinkling of grated mozzarella. Bake for 10 minutes or until the toppings are cooked through and the cheese has melted. Cut into wedges with a pizza slicer and gobble it up!!

Why not try...

Coring out the middle of the pizza and filling it with rocket salad tossed in your favourite dressing like they do in super-flashy restaurants? Looks cool, tastes great and is a fun talking point at the table!

1 onion, sliced

1 tbsp olive oil

600g boneless chicken thighs or breast, cut into chunks

1 tsp cumin seeds

1 garlic clove, finely sliced

1 tsp fresh ginger, finely chopped

400g tin chopped tomatoes

juice and zest of ½ lemon

1 tsp turmeric

1 cinnamon stick

1 tsp paprika

2 tsp ground coriander

100g dried apricots, halved

350g aubergine, cut into small cubes

50g raisins

500ml chicken stock

salt and pepper

1 tbsp honey

1 tbsp freshly chopped parsley

1 tbsp freshly chopped coriander

40g toasted almonds, roughly chopped

To serve:

couscous

natural yoghurt

Oh my, you'll love this one folks. A tagine is a Moroccan steam-cooked-type stew and when you cook this one in your house, you'll feel like you're there (just put a fez on your head to really top it up). If you are lucky enough to own a ceramic tagine dish then you'll be really authentic, but I just use a casserole dish. Here the chicken is cooked in a combination of fruits, spices, herbs and veg – you'll be Ali Baba not to give it a try!

1. Preheat the oven to 170°C/150°C fan/325°F/ Gas mark 3.

2. In a large casserole over a medium heat, soften the onion in the olive oil for 4–5 minutes. Next add the chicken, colouring it all over, then add the cumin seeds, garlic and ginger for 1–2 minutes before adding the tinned tomatoes, lemon zest and juice, turmeric, cinnamon stick, paprika and ground coriander. Literally just stir everything together to combine for a couple of minutes. All that flavour already!

3. Continue topping up the pan – add in the apricots, aubergine, raisins and chicken stock. Give it a little season if you wish, but there's plenty of flavour in there. Bring this all up to a simmer, mixing well.

4. Once simmering, plonk the lid on and bake for a good 45 minutes to steam all that flavour together and soften the chicken. Remove from the oven, take out the cinnamon stick and give everything a stir, then continue to bake, uncovered, for 25–35 minutes until reduced to a consistency of your liking.

5. Remove from the oven again and add the honey, parsley and coriander, stir well and serve up with the almonds sprinkled over. Goes great with couscous and some natural yoghurt mixed with a little extra lemon zest and fresh herbs, if you have any left over.

Why not try...
Mixing up the meat in the tagine? Lamb or beef would be great, or you could load it with vegetables such as sweet potato or squash for a wholesome meat-free equivalent.

Barry's Tip
Keep your eye on the location of the cinnamon stick when mixing so you know where to look when you need to take it out!

Chicken, Aubergine & Apricot TAGINE

Spatchcock
CHICKEN
PARMESAN

about 1.2kg free-range chicken (with no giblets)

3 tbsp olive oil

salt and pepper

1 onion, peeled and finely chopped

1 tbsp red wine vinegar

400g tin chopped tomatoes

2 tbsp chopped fresh basil leaves

pinch of caster sugar

1 mozzarella ball, drained and torn

3 slices of medium-sliced white bread, crusts removed

10 fresh sage leaves

zest of ½ lemon

freshly grated Parmesan, for sprinkling

This recipe brings back memories of summers working in Boston, USA – my first of many tastes of chicken Parmesan came from there. Although sometimes served with ham, this cheesy tomato fest of breadcrumbed chicken will really get you ticking. For this recipe I have made a twist in that I've baked a whole chicken in one tray – so you make the most of that big old bird!

1. Preheat the oven to 200°C/180°C fan/400°F/Gas mark 6.

2. Spatchcock the chicken – snip away the string to free the chicken, flip it onto its belly with its legs towards you and locate the backbone. Snip from the bottom of the backbone (the parson's nose) through the rib bones just to the sides of the bone using kitchen scissors all the way to the top, then turn the chicken over and snip down the other side of the backbone – you should then be able to remove it as one piece. The chicken will now look like a rigid book. It's good practice to remove the breastbone, but for this recipe flip the bird over and push down firmly with your hand. You will hear a lovely crack to break the bone and then it will be done and floppy like a puppet. To neaten the chicken and help it fit into your dish, snip off the feet. Find the joins of the bird, place a sharp knife on top (this is the weakest part) and with a swift bash on the back of the knife the unwanted parts will come away. These parts and the backbone would be good to make stock with.

3. Warm a tablespoon of oil in a frying pan (big enough to fit the chicken). Season the chicken with a little salt and pepper, then brown it on both sides for 7–10 minutes until it turns a lovely mahogany/fake tan colour. Press down on the chicken after putting it in the pan to make sure it cooks evenly. Once you are happy with it, take it out of the pan and leave to rest for the moment.

4. Add another tablespoon of olive oil to the frying pan, then add the onion and sweat for a good 5 minutes until softened. Add the vinegar and mix for a minute or until it has evaporated. Add the chopped tomatoes, basil, sugar, salt and pepper and simmer for 3–4 minutes.

5. Pour the sauce into a 20 x 20cm dish and add blobs of the torn-up mozzarella all around. Sit the chicken in the dish and bake in the oven for 20 minutes.

cont...

6. Meanwhile, clean the frying pan and warm another tablespoon of olive oil. Whizz the bread, sage leaves, lemon zest and a pinch of salt in a food processor until thoroughly combined, then add to the frying pan and fry for about 10 minutes until lightly golden, stirring occasionally and breaking up any clumps that may form. Set aside in a small dish.

7. Once the chicken is done, take it out of the oven and scatter (Mary Poppins style) the breadcrumbs over it and the sauce. Sprinkle freshly grated Parmesan all over – really go to town on it, as much as you like.

8. Bake on the middle shelf of the oven for a further 5 minutes until the Parmesan has melted. Leave to cool slightly before serving with spaghetti or boiled potatoes. I find a cheeky squirt of juice from the lemon zested earlier works a charm too.

Why not try...

Going traditional and bringing ham into the recipe? Get some good-quality stuff from the butcher and dunk torn-off strips into the sauce under the chicken before baking for added texture. Make sure the ham is fully covered by the sauce though.

Barry's Tip

If you are really against the idea of spatchcocking a chicken, you can always buy good-quality chicken pieces in the supermarket, or just ask a butcher to prepare it for you. If you are cooking for one or two people you can also scale down this recipe and just use chicken breasts or thighs; it will work just as well.

Korean COLA CHICKEN

400g skinless chicken thighs

75ml light soy sauce

5cm piece of fresh ginger, peeled and finely chopped

1 garlic clove, peeled and finely chopped

2 tbsp olive oil

330ml can diet cola

To serve:

pan-fried vegetables such as mangetout, spring onions and courgettes

egg-fried rice

Barry's Tip
The longer you can leave the marinade to work into the chicken the better the flavour of the final dish. The deep slits in the chicken will help to get the flavour right into the thighs. Marinate the day before and leave in the fridge overnight for maximum effect.

Chicken thighs are amazing little things, so much more juicy and succulent than a breast, and from what I've found quite under-rated too. Don't let the cola headline get in the way here, this chicken is gorgeous. Cooking the thighs in a soy marinade and cola gives a lovely flavour contrast and Mrs Barry says she can taste tingles on her tongue when eating the finished dish. A quick, quirky and cheap midweek filler that you'll keep coming back to.

1. Using a sharp knife, make a couple of incisions in the chicken thighs and place them in a sealable plastic bag. Pour in the soy sauce, ginger and garlic, seal the bag and massage it all in. Leave to marinate for at least 30 minutes, giving the bag a bit of a shake every so often to get all the flavours working in there.

2. Heat the olive oil in a frying pan over a medium heat. Once hot, remove the chicken pieces from the bag, leaving the marinade in there for the moment, and place in the hot pan, turning and browning the chicken all over for about 3 minutes on each side.

3. Once browned, pour in the marinade from the bag and cook for a further 2 minutes.

4. Next comes the fun part; pour your diet cola into the pan – it will bubble up a little at first, and then begin to simmer. You want to reduce this down over a medium heat, which takes 20–25 minutes. It will seem like nothing is happening at first, and then it will reduce down quickly. During the cooking, continually coat the chicken with the sauce, staining it with flavour and colour, and flipping it every so often to ensure even cooking. Once cooked it will be a lovely rich, deep brown colour with a lovely sweet and sour flavour from the thickened sauce.

5. Serve the chicken with some pan-fried vegetables and egg-fried rice. You can pour the leftover sauce over the chicken for one last glaze.

Why not try...
Serving the egg-fried rice in a coke-can mould? I've done this before and it worked a treat. Once the rice is ready and drained, put it into a can that has had the lid removed, pack it in for a few moments, then tip out onto the plate like a sandcastle!

BEEF & LAMB

⚡

SLOW-ROASTED LAMB
SEARED BEEF & MANGO SALAD
BEEF & RICOTTA STUFFED PASTA SHELLS
PIMPED STEAK & CHEESE SANDWICH
HARISSA LAMB & EGG SUPER PAN
SURF 'N' TURF 'N' OEUF 'N' OOSH
MINTY LAMB MEATBALL TAGLIATELLE
ROAST BEEF IN A GIANT YORKSHIRE PUDDING
BROKEN LASAGNE
BEEF SAN CHOY BAU
CUMIN-RUBBED LAMB WITH MANGO CHUTNEY
7 WAYS WITH MINCED BEEF
LAMB KOFTE STEW
GRIDDLED SOUVLAKI

Slow-ROASTED LAMB

2kg lamb shoulder, bone in

20g fresh rosemary sprigs

10 anchovy fillets, chopped

6 garlic cloves, peeled,
2 cloves cut into fine slices

1 tbsp olive oil

salt and pepper

300ml red wine

1 tbsp balsamic vinegar

To serve:

roast potatoes

Honey Glazed Carrots
(see page 223)

I've not made many roasts on my journey to cook; I guess mainly due to time constraints when I'd get back from work and need a quick fix – but this, folks, is a recipe worth the wait. Lamb shoulder for the size of it is pretty good value and leftovers can be used in so many ways. Combining the shoulder with red wine and rosemary is a popular choice, and here I've added anchovies and balsamic vinegar to take the flavour up another notch.

1. Preheat the oven to 150°C/130°C fan/300°F/Gas mark 2.

2. Using a sharp knife, make some pothole-style slits all over the shoulder and randomly push in the rosemary sprigs, anchovies and garlic slices so the lamb resembles a hedgehog. Put the remaining rosemary sprigs in a large baking tray and scatter in the remaining garlic cloves.

3. Drizzle the lamb with olive oil and season well with salt and pepper. Plonk the lamb into the tray on top of the rosemary and pour in the wine and vinegar. Cover the tray with foil and bake in the oven for a good 3 hours, basting the lamb halfway through with the cooking juices.

4. Take the tray out of the oven, and remove the foil. Increase the oven temperature to 220°C/200°C fan/425°F/Gas Mark 7, then return the lamb, uncovered, to the oven for about 25 minutes or until golden brown all over.

5. Put the lamb on a board to rest for about 20 minutes. Skim off any fat from the tray juices, then serve the lamb with roast potatoes and honey glazed carrots with the pan juices drizzled over the top.

Barry's Tip

If you like, make a gravy with the pan juices, by heating the tray on your hob, adding a little stock and flour and warming through.

Why not try...

Using the leftovers in a lovely crusty sliced baguette with salad to be the envy of your work colleagues?

Seared Beef & MANGO SALAD

400g sirloin steaks

salt and pepper

1 mango, peeled and flesh cut into 2cm chunks

3 little gem lettuce, roughly chopped

15g chopped fresh coriander

15g chopped fresh parsley

15g chopped fresh mint

¼ cucumber, deseeded, halved and thinly sliced

handful of sugar snaps, diagonally sliced

2 spring onions, diagonally sliced

2 tsp sesame seeds, plus extra for sprinkling (optional)

12 cherry tomatoes, halved

juice of 1 lime

fish sauce, to taste

hazelnut oil, to taste

sesame oil, to taste

sugar, to taste

honey, to taste

This is a colourful, texture-filled salad that just makes me smile. I love it as it's so speedy to whip up, is full of my favourite herbs, but has a fruity, juicy element too alongside the strips of sirloin. I don't wanna tell you how to make the dressing – just play around with it and make this salad your own. Yum!

1. Heat a pan over a medium heat and fry the steaks until browned on both sides, about 2–3 minutes per side. Put on a plate, season with salt and pepper and leave to rest.

2. Combine the mango, lettuce, herbs, cucumber, sugar snaps, spring onions, sesame seeds and tomatoes in a large bowl, then using your hands, toss thoroughly to combine.

3. Make a dressing by squirting half the lime juice into a small dish, adding a teaspoon of fish sauce, then topping up with a teaspoon of hazelnut and sesame oils, a pinch of sugar and a teaspoon of honey. Tweak with salt and pepper, plus extra oil, sugar, honey and the remaining lime juice to taste, but don't add any more fish sauce. I like mine a little sweeter so I tend to push the sugar a little more.

4. Slice the steak into diagonal slices, then serve on a stacked bed of the salad with the dressing drizzled over the top. If you like, sprinkle with a few extra sesame seeds – very refreshing.

Why not try...
Making a vegetarian version by adding even more vegetables, such as carrot matchsticks, avocado and bamboo shoots – all would work well.

Barry's Tip
The dressing is what makes the dish your own here, so take the time to tweak it until you are happy with the flavour.

Beef & Ricotta STUFFED PASTA SHELLS

Even before *My Virgin Kitchen*, those extra-large pasta shells in the supermarket would jump out at me and say 'Hey, one day we're gonna make something awesome together'. Well, this is it. Stuffed beef and ricotta pasta shells in a rich passata sauce loaded with cheese and spinach – it just works a charm!

16 conchiglioni large pasta shells (about 120g)

1 tbsp olive oil

400g beef mince

salt and pepper

1 onion, peeled and finely chopped

1 garlic clove, peeled and finely chopped

1 courgette, finely chopped

600g passata

2 handfuls of spinach

3 tbsp grated Parmesan

150g ricotta

12 chopped fresh basil leaves

1 mozzarella ball, torn into little pieces

1. Cook the pasta shells according to the packet instructions until 'al dente'. Take 2 minutes off the cooking instructions and you'll come close. The shells need to hold their shape. Drain, and allow to cool.

2. Meanwhile, heat a frying pan with the olive oil, add the beef and a sprinkling of pepper and cook until browned. Drain most of the fat from the pan and scoop the mince into a bowl. Add the onion to the pan and cook for 3–4 minutes to soften, then add the garlic and courgette and cook for a further 3 minutes. Add the passata, a handful of spinach and some salt and pepper and simmer over a low heat for a good 15 minutes until the sauce is reduced and thickened.

3. Preheat the oven to 200°C/180°C fan/400°F/Gas mark 6.

4. While the sauce reduces, combine the meat, 1 tablespoon of Parmesan, the ricotta, half the fresh basil and a grind of pepper in a mixing bowl. Then fill the pasta shells with the meaty ricotta mixture.

5. Pour two-thirds of the tomato sauce into an ovenproof dish big large enough to take the pasta shells in a single layer, scatter over half the mozzarella pieces, then add the remaining spinach and place the filled pasta shells on top with the open side facing up. Now spoon over the remaining tomato sauce and sprinkle with some more Parmesan. Finally, top with the remaining mozzarella, more basil leaves and season with salt and pepper. Try to coat the pasta edges well, to prevent too much exposure to the heat.

6. Bake for 15–20 minutes or until the cheese is golden and bubbly.

Barry's Tip

Don't panic if your pasta isn't 'al dente', it'll just be harder to fill the shells. Better to cook the pasta fully for sure!

Why not try...

Switching up the meat here with some shredded chicken? Poach chicken breasts until cooked through and shred with a fork.

300g sirloin steak

salt and pepper

2 tbsp olive oil

1 small onion, peeled and sliced finely into strips

4 small mushrooms, thinly sliced

2 small handfuls of spinach

1 tsp double cream

800g pack of focaccia bread mix, prepared as per packet instructions

4 thin slices of Cheddar cheese

1 egg, beaten (optional)

To serve:

rocket salad

This combination of steak and cheese reminds me of travelling across America with Mrs Barry on a train, as nearly every main station we stopped off at had some sort of steak and cheese combo. In this recipe sirloin steak is wrapped in pre-made dough and stuffed with a good match of creamy mushrooms, spinach and, of course, cheese. You'll love this!

1. Preheat the oven to 200°C/180°C fan/400°F/Gas mark 6 (or according to the dough instructions) and line a baking tray with baking parchment.

2. Season the steak with pepper. Heat half the oil in a separate pan until hot and brown the steak on both sides for 3–4 minutes. A 4-minute steak should be well done, but bear in mind it is going in the oven after it's wrapped. Set aside to rest.

3. Meanwhile, heat the remaining oil in a frying pan over a medium heat, add the onion and cook until golden, a good 10 minutes. After 5 minutes, tip in the mushrooms and fry until softened. In the final minute, add the spinach and wilt. Take off the heat and pour in the cream and 2 teaspoons of any steak juices. Mix through, then allow to cool.

4. Divide the dough into three and roll out one-third until it is 5mm thick. Thinly spread half the spinach mixture in the centre of the dough. Cover with 2 slices of Cheddar, pat the steak dry with kitchen paper and sit it on top. Repeat these steps in reverse – top the steak with the remaining cheese, then the spinach mixture, adding extra seasoning if you wish.

5. Wrap the steak neatly and tightly until fully encased in the dough, cutting away any excess with a sharp knife – do not overlap the dough or it won't cook all the way through. Brush the joins with water and gently press to seal. Put on the lined tray, seal-side down, and bake for 15 minutes or according to the dough packet instructions until golden brown and cooked through. If you want a deeper colour, brush the parcel with beaten egg halfway through baking.

6. Serve the parcel, sliced at angles, with a rocket salad.

Why not try...

Making a simple horseradish mayo for dunking the sandwich into? Or spread a little horseradish on the steaks before wrapping up for an added kick!

Barry's Tip

Use up the leftover dough to make a focaccia loaf, or multiply the ingredients and make more pimped sandwiches!

Harissa Lamb &

EGG SUPER PAN

Is it a bird? Is it a plane? No. I just love this dish, it's a little kinky, I'm not gonna lie, but you can tone it down. Lamb mince is cooked up with onions and button mushrooms and whirled around in harissa and passata before cracking eggs on top to cook in a super-hero pan party – deeelish.

500g minced lamb

1 onion, diced

1 yellow pepper, deseeded and diced

100g button mushrooms, halved

2 tbsp harissa paste

400g passata

salt and pepper

4 medium eggs

4 or 5 fresh chives

To serve:

rice

1. In a frying pan with a lid (ideally transparent) over a medium heat, dry-fry the lamb until browned, then drain off most of the fat. Add the onion and cook for a couple more minutes, then add the pepper and button mushrooms for 3–4 minutes to soften.

2. Next, spoon in the harissa paste – use a little less if you want it milder – and stir to coat. Top up with the passata, a good seasoning of salt and pepper, then simmer for 10 minutes to reduce slightly. We don't want the surface too wet for the next step.

3. Make four indents in the mixture and crack an egg into each one, cover and cook for around 7–8 minutes or until the eggs are set to your liking, but keep your eye on them. Spoon straight out of the pan onto plates, season, then snip some chives over the top. Serve with rice.

Why not try...

Adding some cubed pancetta to the mixture for a little saltiness and texture. Swap the lamb for minced beef or pork.

Barry's Tip

If you don't have a lidded frying pan you can always place your frying pan under a grill instead until cooked through.

Surf 'n' Turf 'n' OEUF 'n' OOSH

4 smoked bacon rashers

salt and pepper

2 fillet steaks, at room temperature

vegetable oil

2 pineapple rings

olive oil

100g raw king prawns

knob of butter

¼ onion, finely diced

1 tbsp white wine

1 tbsp single cream

handful of chopped fresh parsley

1 tsp mustard powder

2 eggs

Barry's Tip
Check with your butcher or cooking instructions on the steak package for cooking times if you are uncertain.

This is a little treat for two, a treat in that we are using fillet steak, which isn't the cheapest, and also that this is one heck of a combo, so you won't want to make it every day. Here surf (prawns), turf (steak), oeuf (fried egg) and ooosh (pineapple & bacon!?!) are brought together in a creamy wine sauce. This recipe has a lovely ranging layer of textures as you gobble your way through it – hope you enjoy!

1. Place the bacon under a medium grill and cook until crispy and lightly charred, turning halfway through cooking. Leave to one side while you crack on with the other steps.

2. Give the steaks a little rub with vegetable oil and season, then pan-fry to your liking – I normally do about 3–4 minutes each side turning a few times for medium-rare in a really hot pan. Plonk on a plate to rest.

3. Meanwhile get a griddle pan nice and hot and place your pineapple slices on it, cooking to get brown griddle lines on both sides. Set aside. Immediately add a little olive oil to the pan with the prawns and cook for a minute either side to turn pink.

4. Melt the knob of butter over a medium heat in a saucepan and once it starts to bubble add the onion and cook to soften, stirring from time to time, for 4–5 minutes. Tip in the white wine and simmer for 2 minutes before topping up with the cream, some chopped parsley, mustard powder, juice from the rested steaks and a grind of pepper. Stir, then tip in the prawns, coating them in the sauce. Keep this on a low heat while you do the eggs.

5. In the pan that you cooked the steak in, add a small glug of oil and fry your eggs, seasoning the white if you wish before it sets.

6. Once ready, plonk the steaks on a plate, spoon on some prawns with the creamy sauce, top with a griddled pineapple ring, a fried egg, then the crispy bacon strips. Season and scatter over some extra parsley, if you wish, and serve with peas and homemade wedges to make it even more fillin' – good stuff!

Why not try...
Switching up the steak and omitting the bacon and going with gammon, for that classic ham, egg and pineapple combo.

Minty
LAMB MEATBALL TAGLIATELLE

500g lamb mince

1 heaped tsp ground cumin

1 garlic clove, peeled and finely chopped

½ onion, peeled and finely chopped

salt and pepper

25g fresh mint, finely chopped, set a little aside for sprinkling

50g pine nuts

olive oil, for cooking

250g chestnut mushrooms, thinly sliced

284ml tub light single cream

80g kale

1 tbsp wholegrain mustard

150ml vegetable stock

grated Parmesan, to taste

500g fresh tagliatelle

I have been trying to find a way to get my fascination of lamb and mint into a lovely recipe that isn't too manly shoved in a bun, and Mrs Barry reckons this is the one. Homemade minty meatballs drenched in a creamy sauce, served with fresh tagliatelle and toasted pine nuts – deeeeeeelicious!

1. First make the lamb meatballs. In a mixing bowl, break up the mince a bit with a spatula, then add the cumin, garlic, onion, pinch of salt, grind of pepper and most of the mint and mix well to combine. Get your hands in there and mix thoroughly. Roll small portions of the mix into ping-pong-sized balls and arrange on a chopping board. Make sure your balls are the same size for even cooking. If you aren't cooking them immediately, refrigerate.

2. Heat a small frying pan over a medium heat, add the pine nuts and toast briefly – a max of 5 minutes – until browned, giving the pan a shake as you go, then set aside.

3. Heat a drop of oil in a larger pan, add the meatballs and cook for a good 10 minutes, pushing them around gently and making sure they are browning evenly. Transfer to kitchen paper to drain.

4. Add the mushrooms to the meatball pan and cook for 4–5 minutes to soften. You shouldn't need any more oil. Return the meatballs to the pan, tip in the cream, kale, mustard, most of the toasted pine nuts, vegetable stock, another good grind of pepper and a sprinkle of Parmesan and simmer over a low heat for 10–15 minutes to thicken slightly, stirring gently with a spatula.

5. Bring a pan of water to the boil, then lower the heat and add the tagliatelle. Cook according to the packet instructions, about 4 minutes.

6. Drain the pasta and serve piled on plates with the meatball mixture and sauce on top. Add extra sauce, if you like, then top with more grated Parmesan, pepper, any remaining toasted pine nuts and a sprinkling of the leftover mint.

Why not try...

You can mix the pasta in with the sauce prior to serving if you prefer. A drop of white wine would be nice added to the sauce, but you'll lose a little of the minty edge.

Barry's Tip

The fresh pasta won't take long to cook. If you are using dried pasta you will need to get this on to boil earlier in the recipe.

Roast Beef
IN A GIANT YORKSHIRE PUDDING

1.5kg rolled beef sirloin

salt and pepper

2 tbsp mustard powder

1 heaped tsp mixed herbs

eggs (see tip below)

plain flour (see tip below)

semi-skimmed milk (see tip below)

1 tbsp olive oil

To serve:

vegetables of your choice

gravy

Barry's Tip
The egg, milk and flour ratio is measured in volume. Crack the eggs into a glass first to get an indication of the level, then add the milk and flour to the same height. I used 3 eggs in my cake tin, but you can get away with 2 if you are using, say, a sandwich tin.

You may have seen those microwave meals in the freezer aisles in supermarkets where a huge Yorkshire pudding is filled with the dinner you eat. Well, it's actually kinda easy to make your own from home and fill it with whatever you like (I have put curry and chips in one before!). Give this a go – the beef is great, but if you prefer you could serve it traditionally.

1. Preheat the oven to 220°C/200°C fan/425°F/Gas mark 7.

2. Rub the beef generously with salt and pepper, then put in the oven for about 5–7 minutes until the outside is coloured.

3. Meanwhile, mix the mustard powder and herbs together in a bowl. When the beef is browned, work the mustard mixture over the beef.

4. Return the beef to the oven. Depending on the weight of your beef the cooking time will vary. As a rough guide, it's about 15–17 minutes per 450g for medium or 20–22 minutes for well done, plus an extra 15 or 22 minutes respectively. Regardless of what you choose, after 20 minutes turn the oven down to 180°C/160°C fan/350°F/Gas mark 4 and cook for the remaining calculated time. Once done, cover in foil and leave to rest on a board for 30 minutes.

5. Meanwhile, prepare the batter for the Yorkshire pudding and cook the vegetables. Whisk the eggs, flour, milk and a pinch of salt together until well combined. Make sure that there are no lumps. Set aside.

6. When the beef is done, increase the oven temperature to 200°C/180°C fan/400°F/Gas mark 6. Put the olive oil into a high-sided round cake tin and put it in the oven for 5 minutes until hot. Tip in the batter to cover the base of the tin, then return to the oven until risen and golden brown, about 15–17 minutes. The pudding can go from brown to black fast, so keep your eye on it.

7. Take the pudding out of the oven, press down the middle with the back of a spoon, then load up with the meat, vegetables and gravy – delicious.

Why not try...
Making mini versions of this? Put the batter into muffin tins and put your filling in the middle at cool angles for a quirky approach!

Broken
LASAGNE

There's nothing better than a good old lasagne, and the cool thing about this one is that it uses leftover pasta you have lying around in your cupboard – and if you're anything like me, you'll have a good combo. This recipe works well with traditional lasagne sheets too – it's a real meaty pasta treat.

2 tbsp olive oil

1 red onion, peeled and diced

2 garlic cloves, peeled and chopped

½ carrot, peeled and grated

2 celery sticks, trimmed and diced

500g beef mince

2 tbsp tomato purée

1 bay leaf

1 heaped tsp dried oregano

400g tin chopped tomatoes

40ml water

2 tbsp red wine (optional)

1 beef stock cube

300g mixed pasta (whatever you have lying about, not fresh though!)

1. Heat the olive oil in a pan over a medium heat. When hot, add the onion and sweat for a couple of minutes before adding the garlic, carrot and celery. Let it all cook together for a good 5 minutes.

2. Increase the heat and tip in the mince, hacking it up with your spatula to break down any meaty lumps. Add the tomato purée, bay leaf and oregano and continue to fry for a further 2 minutes.

3. Pour in the tomatoes, water, wine (if using) and crumble in the stock cube, giving it a good old stir. Bring to the boil, reduce the heat and simmer for a good 40 minutes. If the mixture starts to look dry add a little water, but don't make it a lake!

4. Meanwhile, make the cheese sauce. Melt the butter in a saucepan, add the flour and stir it in until it is a yellowy paste, then cook gently for 2 minutes.

5. Start adding the milk, bit by bit, whisking with a hand whisk all the time to make sure there are no lumps. Don't worry if there are – you can get rid of them with more whisking!

6. Once all the milk has been added, keep stirring over a medium heat until it thickens.

7. When the sauce is smooth and silky, lower the heat and cook gently for about 5 minutes. Add the Cheddar cheese and stir until melted into your sauce.

8. Preheat the oven to 190°C/170°C fan/375°F/Gas mark 5.

For the cheese sauce:

butter

plain flour

ml whole milk

100g strong Cheddar cheese, grated

25g Parmesan, grated

To serve:

garlic bread (see page 229)

side salad

9. Drop the pasta shapes into the meat sauce, stir, then simmer for about 5 minutes before tipping half of the pasta mixture into a roasting dish. Top with half the cheese sauce, then tip the remaining pasta mixture on top and finish with another layer of the remaining cheese sauce.

10. Top the mixture with a scattering of Parmesan. Bake in the oven for about 30 minutes until the top is nicely browned and the pasta is cooked through. Serve up with some garlic bread and a side salad.

Why not try...

Once you've made this a few times, make a basic white sauce and stir it through with the meaty pasta mixture before baking, to add another colour/taste dimension.

Barry's Tip

Let the mixture simmer for as long as you can, because this really helps to work the flavours all around. You can also make ahead and store in the fridge for 1–2 days.

Beef
SAN CHOY BAU

1 tbsp groundnut oil

2 garlic cloves, peeled and finely chopped

2.5cm piece of fresh ginger, peeled and finely chopped

500g minced beef

5 tbsp oyster sauce

3 tbsp soy sauce

150g beansprouts

1 carrot, peeled and finely sliced

2 spring onions, sliced

1 onion, peeled and finely chopped

80g water chestnuts, sliced

2 red chillies, deseeded and finely chopped

4 dried shiitake mushrooms, soaked in cold water for 10 minutes, drained, dried and thinly sliced

1 heaped tsp sugar

salt and pepper

4 little gem lettuce

I have tried to come up with something turn my fascination of wrapping things in tortillas to using lettuce leaves, giving the dish a refreshing, crunchy vibe. This recipe does it, a kickin' combo of veg and beef mince, piled into little gem lettuce leaves; it's super-good, super-easy to make your own... Enjoy, and remember to share!

1. Heat the groundnut oil in a wok over a high heat. Once the oil is hot, add the garlic and ginger and stir-fry for 30 seconds. Add the beef and brown for a good 4–5 minutes, hacking up with a spatula to break it down if necessary.

2. Tip away any excess fat from the beef, then add the oyster and soy sauces (see tip below), beansprouts, carrot, spring onions, onion, water chestnuts, chillies, mushrooms and a pinch of sugar and stir-fry for a good 8–10 minutes until the vegetables and beef are cooked. It's important here to keep the mixture as dry as you can.

3. Taste to make sure you are happy with the flavour and season as necessary, then spoon the mixture into the little gem lettuce leaves. Very addictive indeedy!

Why not try...
Omitting the beef mince to make it vegetarian, or try with prawns or chicken?

Barry's Tip
The oyster and soy sauce quantities can be tweaked as you go – you may want to add them gradually to taste and then add more if needed. I like mine a little stronger than the above, but this still has a good kick.

Cumin-Rubbed LAMB WITH MANGO CHUTNEY

1 tsp salt

1 tsp pepper

2 tsp ground cumin

6 lamb cutlets (about 560g)

1 heaped tbsp mango chutney

2 tsp red wine vinegar

2 tbsp water

½ tin chickpeas, drained

2 handfuls of mixed salad leaves

Barry's Tip

We are 'dry rubbing' the cumin and seasoning in here, but if you fancy it you can always add a small mix of olive oil – this 'wet rub' will stick to the meat better.

A lovely light, quick, cheap midweek meal that means you can get it made, get fed and maybe make one of the naughty desserts in this book to make up for it and not feel guilty. Here, lamb is rubbed with a cumin seasoning and then served in a nest of mixed leaf chickpea salad and drizzled in mango dressing. Works great as a lunch too – hope you give it a try!

1. Preheat the grill until nice and hot. Meanwhile, mix the salt, pepper and cumin together, then rub the mix all over the lamb.

2. Place the lamb under the grill and cook for about 4 minutes on both sides until lovely and golden with a little cumin shade to it.

3. Meanwhile, make the dressing. Mix the chutney, vinegar and water together in a bowl. Taste and tweak to your liking – use the water to calm it, vinegar for zing and chutney for sweetness – until you're happy.

4. Leave the cooked lamb to rest. Meanwhile, put the chickpeas and mixed salad leaves in a large bowl, top with some of the dressing and mix together to combine and coat.

5. Serve the lamb with the chickpea salad and drizzle over any remaining dressing.

Why not try...

Whacking it all together into a delicious ciabatta for a grab-and-go lamb and chickpea bite?

7 Ways WITH MINCED BEEF

One thing I've learnt about minced beef, there's always something cool you can do with it to freshen things up. Here are a few options – there are loads more, plus you can tweak these a lot. I've skipped out some personal favourites here, like fajitas, but hopefully this'll help you out if you ever find yourself staring longingly at a pack of mince in a supermarket getting odd looks. Just me? Oh, ok.

A sample base mix

In a saucepan over a medium heat, sweat an onion in a little olive oil until translucent, then add a garlic clove and cook for 1 minute. Top up with a squeeze of tomato purée, stirring for another minute. Then chuck in 500g mince and brown fully, stirring from time to time. Finally, add a tin of chopped tomatoes and a pinch each of sugar, salt and pepper to taste.

1. Cottage pie

Cook one stick of celery and carrot with the onion, then when the garlic is added, pour in 150ml red wine and reduce by two-thirds. Replace the tomatoes with beef stock. Tip into a casserole dish and top with mashed potato and grated cheese, and sprinkle over salt and pepper. Bake until golden brown.

2. Spaghetti Bolognese

Add carrot and celery to the base mix then add 150ml red wine, a few halved mushrooms and cherry tomatoes and reduce by two-thirds. Add mixed herbs, then serve with cooked spaghetti, grated Parmesan and some chopped fresh basil.

3. Lasagne

Use the Bolognese as the meat base. Make a white sauce by melting 30g butter in a pan on low heat, stirring in 30g flour and cooking for 1 minute. Add 600ml milk and seasoning off the heat, stir until smooth.

cont...

(4)

(5)

(6)

(7)

Put back over the heat to thicken slightly, bringing it to a boil. Lay fresh lasagne sheets in a baking dish, add a little Bolognese mixture, sprinkle Parmesan on top, then add a little white sauce. Repeat these steps to finish with white sauce, then top with Parmesan and torn mozzarella.

4. *Mince stroganoff*

Add mushrooms with the garlic and fry to achieve a golden colour. Add 1 teaspoon of paprika and cook for 1 minute. Add 50ml brandy and reduce by two-thirds. Replace the tomato purée and tomatoes with a beef stock cube, a little water and a shake of Worcestershire sauce, cook. Finish with soured cream, flat-leaf parsley and lemon juice. Seasoning to your liking.

5. *Quesadilla*

Add red, yellow and green peppers, red chilli (optional) while frying the onion and omit the chopped tomatoes and sugar. Spread tomato salsa over a tortilla wrap, top with the mince mix, then add sliced spring onions and chopped coriander. Top with grated Cheddar and another tortilla. Heat some oil in a frying pan and fry the tortilla sandwich on both sides for 2–3 minutes until crisp, the cheese is melted and the filling heated through.

6. *Chilli*

Add 1 teaspoon hot smoked paprika to the garlic-onion mix and a beef stock cube with 2 teaspoons of chilli paste. Add a tin of rinsed kidney beans with chopped tomatoes, sprinkle on a little oregano and serve with soured cream, tortilla chips and salsa.

7. *Curried mince*

Add 1 tablespoon of curry powder (your preferred strength) with the garlic and use an equivalent measure of beef stock instead of tomatoes. Omit the sugar and sweeten with mango chutney. Garnish with coriander, serve with rice and a dollop of natural yoghurt on top.

Lamb
KOFTE STEW

For the kofte:

500g minced lamb

1 small onion, peeled and diced

1½ tsp ground cumin

1 tsp ground coriander

¼ tsp ground cinnamon

½ tsp turmeric

½ tsp cayenne pepper

2 tbsp chopped fresh coriander

1 tbsp chopped fresh mint

For the stew:

olive oil, for cooking

1 carrot, peeled and diced

1 onion, peeled and finely sliced

1 garlic clove, peeled and chopped

1 tsp ground cumin

This is a lovely dish – I've rolled up lamb a few times in this book but in this recipe mini lamb koftes are dunked into a lovely tomato stew which has a little punch of cumin and cardamom. It's a real winner and with a swirl of the tzatziki swirled through it can be made to look pretty flashy too.

1. Mix all the kofte ingredients in a bowl. Get your hands in there, roll up your sleeves and mix thoroughly until all the ingredients are evenly combined. Take golf-ball-sized pieces of the mixture and roll out into stubby cigar shapes (roughly 16). Once all the mixture has been used, put the kofte in the fridge until needed.

2. Make the stew by heating a little olive oil in a pan over a medium heat. Add the carrot and onion and fry for 5–7 minutes, then add the garlic, cumin, turmeric, tomato purée and cardamom seeds, stir and cook for a further 2 minutes. Add the chopped tomatoes and water, crumble in the stock cubes, then season and simmer for about 25 minutes, stirring occasionally.

3. Meanwhile, make the tzatziki. Grate the cucumber, put in a sieve with a pinch of salt and leave to drain for 20 minutes. Pat dry with kitchen paper, then mix with the yoghurt, garlic, cumin, lemon juice and seasoning. Add these flavourings gradually to taste if you prefer. Chill in the fridge until needed.

1 tsp turmeric

1 tsp tomato purée

3 cardamom pods, bashed seeds only

2 x 400g tins chopped tomatoes

250ml water

2 chicken stock cubes

salt and pepper

boiled potatoes, to serve (optional)

For the tzatziki:

1 cucumber, deseeded

250g Greek yoghurt

1 garlic clove, peeled and crushed

1 heaped tsp ground cumin

juice of 1 lemon

salt and pepper

4. Heat a griddle pan over a medium heat and fry the koftes until browned on each side. Once done, dunk them into the stew and continue to cook for a further 15 minutes. Season the stew as you like, perhaps add a little more cumin if you want a bit more edge.

5. Serve the stew in bowls with the tzatziki swirled through and a little leftover chopped coriander (or even some reserved cucumber works too!) and salt and pepper sprinkled over the top. This goes great with some boiled potatoes – warming and lovely!

Why not try...

Turning the dish into a pie? Combine the lamb with the stew and top with a lid of mashed potato, then bake until browned.

Barry's Tip

Feel free to mix up the seasoning to your liking. It's a slightly less minty approach, but the tomato tang works a charm.

500g lean diced lamb, lightly seasoned

3 tbsp olive oil

zest and juice 2 lemons, (have another one lying about for tweaks)

2 garlic cloves, peeled and finely chopped

1 red onion, peeled and diced

1 yellow pepper, deseeded and diced

1 courgette, diced

½ tsp oregano (or Greek seasoning if you can get, as it is amazing)

½ tsp dried mixed herbs

120ml red wine

salt and pepper

8 pittas/flatbreads, toasted

sweet chilli sauce

small pot of Greek yoghurt

½ red lettuce, cut into strips

100g cherry tomatoes, cut in half

¼ cucumber, deseeded and cut into mini chunks

a little chopped fresh mint, for sprinkling

cubed feta cheese

Sexy Greek fast-food-style kebabs right here and if you make ahead, they can be cooked in a flash! Here the lamb and vegetables are marinated in a zesty red wine marinade, griddled and packed into a crunchy pitta full of textured flavoured fun – so, so, so good. The ingredients list looks quite long, but it's honestly so easy – I recommend making double the amount to keep ahead for when you're feeling peckish.

1. Put the lamb, olive oil, zest of both lemons and the juice of 1, the garlic, onion, pepper, courgette, herbs, red wine and a grind of pepper together in a sealable plastic bag or a bowl and mix well to combine. Seal the bag or cover the bowl and leave to marinate in the fridge for at least an hour.

2. When you're ready to cook the lamb, get a griddle pan nice and hot over a medium heat, add the marinated meat and vegetables with just a little of the marinade to the pan and griddle for about 7–8 minutes, turning over as you go until the lamb is browned all over and cooked through. Check to make sure that the lamb is completely cooked before removing from the heat. You can push the veg to the side of the griddle to keep warm while you cook the lamb in batches.

3. Split open the toasted pittas and load them with the lamb, peppers, courgette, onion, sweet chilli sauce, yoghurt, lettuce, tomatoes and cucumber with a little mint and feta over the top – oh wow! This goes great with some rice, couscous or quinoa.

Why not try…
Any leftovers will make amazing sandwiches and you can use other meats like chicken or steak chunks, or make it vegetarian by using aubergine and bringing in some pineapple and mushrooms.

Barry's Tip
The longer you leave the lamb to marinate the better it will be; overnight will really make a difference.

Griddled
SOUVLAKI

HAM, PORK & BACON

FIVE-SPICE ROAST PORK BELLY
ASPARAGUS, MINT & PANCETTA SOUP
BRUSSELS SPROUT & PANCETTA FUSILLI
GRILLED PORK & PEAR WITH WALNUT SALAD
IN A BLUE CHEESE DRESSING
BANGERS & MUSTARD MASH CASSEROLE
OH AH QUINOA SALAD
PORK TENDERLOIN SCHNITZEL
TOAD TARTE TATIN
BBQ PULLED PORK CIABATTAS
PROSCIUTTO, STRAWBERRY & MELON SALAD
BACON RIGATONI CARBONARA
PARMA HAM, ARTICHOKE & ASPARAGUS TART

Five-Spice ROAST PORK BELLY

750g pork belly, left in fridge uncovered to dry skin, then patted dry

- - - - - - - - - - - - - - - - - - -

1 garlic clove, crushed

- - - - - - - - - - - - - - - - - - -

2 tsp five spice

- - - - - - - - - - - - - - - - - - -

salt and pepper (optional)

Barry's Tip

If you're not happy with the crackling after baking you can always whack it under the grill briefly to crisp up more, then set up your own pork-scratching business on the side!

I'd not used five spice often before trying this recipe, in fact to me five spice sounds more like a nickname for the Spice Girls – but, viva forever, this is an absolute stunner. The ingredients are minimal and it will make a lot of people envious of the smell from your kitchen, let alone the slightly Asian vibe going on. Make sure you give it a good rub all over and you'll love the colour on this.

1. Preheat the oven to 220°C/200°C fan/425°F/Gas mark 7. Finely score the pork fat in diagonals, then do the same the other way to create diamond shapes on the surface. Carefully pour over a little boiling water from a kettle and watch the diamonds grow a little, which'll really help the crackling!

2. Pat dry the belly, then rub the garlic and five spice all over, staining it with colour, and season, if you like. Cook in the oven for 20–25 minutes to get the crackling lovely and crisp initially.

3. Lower the oven temperature slightly to 200°C/180°C fan/400°F/Gas mark 6 and bake for a further 45–50 minutes to cook through.

4. Let the meat rest for 10 minutes before carving up and serving with vegetables of your choice.

Why not try...

If you're not in a hurry, lower the heat after crisping the top to 140°C/120°C fan/275°F/Gas mark 1 and slow-roast for a good 2 hours.

Asparagus, MINT & PANCETTA SOUP

I used to hate asparagus; I'm not sure why but I think it just looks weird, like a green tickling stick. However, there's so much you can do with it and it cooks so quickly. Here I've made it the main part of a yummy minty soup with a little pancetta for company.

knob of butter

150g pancetta chunks (or sliced bacon)

500g asparagus spears, rough stalks snipped off, spears cut into chunks

1 onion, peeled and sliced

1 garlic clove, peeled and chopped

300ml milk (use cream if feeling naughty)

300ml vegetable stock

handful of chopped fresh mint, plus extra to garnish

salt and pepper

To serve:

good bread

Barry's Tip
If you want larger pieces of pancetta in the final dish, remove them before blending with the other ingredients.

1. Heat a large saucepan over a medium heat, add the butter and leave until melted and bubbling. Add the pancetta and cook for about 3 minutes. Next, tip in the asparagus and onion and cook for about 5–7 minutes to soften. The garlic will be looking lonely, so add this in for the final minute. Pick out a little bit of the pancetta/veg and set aside for the garnish (this is optional, but it makes it look sexy).

2. Pour in the milk, stock and mint and season well while bringing everything to the boil.

3. Carefully transfer the mixture to a blender and whizz until it's all combined and smooth.

4. Serve with a little extra fresh mint sprinkled over, the reserved pancetta/veg, seasoning and, like most soups, with some decent bread, maybe some focaccia.

Why not try...
You could give the soup more depth by adding some kale or cabbage.

Brussels Sprout & PANCETTA FUSILLI

1 tbsp olive oil

300g Brussels sprouts, outer leaves peeled, trimmed and quartered

1 onion, peeled and finely chopped

160g cubed pancetta

pepper

70ml white wine

300g cherry tomatoes, sliced into quarters

2 garlic cloves, peeled and finely chopped

500g fresh fusilli pasta

handful of fresh basil, chopped, plus a few extra leaves to garnish

50g Parmesan, grated, plus extra for sprinkling

This is a very light pasta dish which uses that ingredient most people only think about around Christmas time – Brussels sprouts! They combine really well with the cherry tomatoes and pancetta to give you a pasta dish that fills you up but isn't weighed down with a creamy sauce. There's the right balance of flavour in here to carry it home. If you're after a more refreshing pasta dish, this is the one to put your own twist on.

1. Heat a frying pan over a medium heat, add the olive oil, then tip in the Brussels sprouts and cook for a good 7–8 minutes until starting to brown. At this point, tip in the onion and pancetta and cook for a good 6–8 minutes to soften and add colour. Stir with a spatula from time to time and season with a little pepper.

2. When everything is browned nicely, add the wine and let it bubble for 30 seconds, then add the tomatoes and garlic and cook for another 5 minutes. Squish the tomatoes and hack up the sprouts at this stage to mix everything thoroughly.

3. Meanwhile, cook the pasta according to the packet instructions (normally 4 minutes). Once the pancetta mixture is ready, drain the pasta, reserving 2 tablespoons of the cooking water, then tip the pasta and water into the pan with the pancetta. Add the chopped basil and grated Parmesan and season with pepper to taste. Cook for 2 more minutes, then stir well but don't be too rough as you don't want to break the pasta.

4. Serve sprinkled generously with more grated cheese, pepper and garnish with basil leaves – super-smashing stuff!

Why not try...

If you do want a little texture, throw in 2 tablespoons of crème fraîche after mixing in the pasta – Mrs Barry prefers it without, though, so that means I have to also.

Barry's Tip

Make sure your sprouts are cooked and softened throughout before moving on – you don't want any embarrassing crunchy sprout moments!

Grilled Pork & PEAR WITH WALNUT SALAD IN A BLUE CHEESE DRESSING

2 pork chops

salt and pepper

1 tbsp light brown sugar (optional)

1 ripe pear, peeled and halved

40g Stilton cheese, rind removed

1 tsp celery salt

50ml crème fraîche

1 tbsp warm water

6 tsp Worcestershire sauce, or to taste

2 good handfuls of rocket leaves

1 tbsp roughly chopped walnuts

Some of you may be aware of my old fear of blue cheese; I made a video trying to overcome it directly and just couldn't stomach it straight. But when it's melted or merged with other flavours it's actually pretty good. In this recipe pork chops and pears are grilled together and stacked up with a lovely salad coated in the dressing and topped with bashed walnuts – the flavours combined on a fork are truly amazing. Hope you give this one a try, even if you're not a blue cheese fan!

1. Preheat the grill to Medium–High and season the pork chops with a little salt and pepper. You can sprinkle the light brown sugar onto the pear if you wish.

2. Grill the pork chops and pear for 7–8 minutes on one side, then flip over and cook for the same time on the other side. Keep an eye on the pear to ensure it doesn't burn. The pork should be well browned on both sides and the pears lovely and softened. Leave the pork and pear to rest for a few minutes.

3. Meanwhile, whizz the cheese, celery salt and crème fraîche in a blender, gradually adding the warm water and Worcestershire sauce to taste. (The water needs to be warm to help break down the cheese a little.) The quantities give a tangy dressing with a kick of blue cheese.

4. Slice both the pear slices in half again so you have quarters. Sit the pork chops on plates, top each with 2 pear quarters stacked over each other, then scatter over the rocket leaves with the chopped walnuts and a lovely drizzle of the dressing.

Why not try...

Mixing up the fruit a bit? Perhaps keep the peel on the pear for a yummy rippled skin or grill it alongside some pineapple rings/peach halves.

Barry's Tip

You may want to keep the pear a little firmer; throw it in for the last half of the pork grilling time and it'll turn out delicious.

Bangers
& MUSTARD MASH CASSEROLE

8 sausages of your choice

1 tbsp olive oil

1 onion, peeled and sliced

1 leek, trimmed and sliced

1 heaped tsp paprika

4–5 mushrooms, sliced

1 garlic clove, peeled and minced

1 large or 2 small carrots, peeled and cut into chunks

1 large or 2 small parsnips, peeled and cut into chunks

400g jar passata

splash of Worcestershire sauce

1 tsp dried oregano

400ml beef stock

salt and pepper

1kg medium potatoes, peeled and quartered

50g butter

3 tbsp milk

2 tbsp wholegrain mustard (optional)

25g grated Cheddar cheese, for sprinkling (optional)

chopped fresh basil leaves, to garnish

One of my favourite dinners in the whole wide world has got to be sausage casserole – I find it so comforting and filling. In this recipe we make a lovely casserole and top it with a lid of mashed potato to create a brilliant crowd pleaser.

1. Cook the sausages in the olive oil in a frying pan over a medium heat for about 8–10 minutes or until golden all over. Set aside to rest.

2. Add the onions and leek to the frying pan (there shouldn't be a need for any more oil at this stage) and fry them for a good 10 minutes until they start to caramelise a little. Tip in the paprika, mushrooms and garlic, mix well and cook for 2 minutes more.

3. Add the carrots and parsnips to the pan, then snip the sausages into mini chunks, add them to the pan and mix together.

4. Add the passata, Worcestershire sauce and dried oregano and mix well. Pour in the stock, season with pepper and mix well. Leave to simmer for a good 30 minutes, stirring from time to time.

5. Meanwhile, cook the potatoes in a separate pan of boiling water until soft, about 15–20 minutes. Drain, return to the pan and mash together with the butter, milk and mustard, if using. Season generously and mash until smooth.

6. If you want to serve the casserole and mash separately, congratulations – you've just made dinner! However, to complete the look, preheat the grill to Medium. Spoon the sausage mixture into an ovenproof dish and top with the mashed potato. Spread it carefully with a spatula, then make some patterns with a fork if you're feeling artistic. If you are using cheese, sprinkle this over the top and season well.

7. Grill until the potato topping is crisp and golden brown. Serve with chopped basil leaves scattered over the top.

Why not try...

Bulking out the mixture by adding chorizo sausage, bacon or kidney beans? There's really no end to what can be added.

Oh Ah QUINOA SALAD

180g quinoa

salt and pepper

200g pineapple pieces (there's no need to cut in half) juice not needed, just drink it – yum!

1 avocado, peeled, stoned and cut into small cubes

1 carrot, peeled and sliced thinly using a potato peeler

1 mozzarella ball, torn into pieces

6–8 slices of Parma ham, torn in half

½ cucumber, deseeded and cut into small chunks

1 red onion, peeled and finely chopped

good handful of fresh parsley, finely chopped

good handful of fresh mint, finely sliced

juice of 2 lemons

juice of 2 limes

2 tbsp olive oil

dash of honey

Quinoa (pronounced 'keen wah') has become a bit of a buzz food in recent times, it's fluffy and super-easy to use, like a new rice on the block. Here I'm using it in a refreshing salad with some delicious light favourites alongside. You can pack this baby out anyway you like, but if you want a light fill, this should do the trick – you'll be saying 'oh ah' like a true Bristolian in no time!

1. First of all give the quinoa a good wash through a sieve to take away some of its bitter coating. Bring it to the boil in 480ml water with a pinch of salt, then lower the heat and simmer for 15–20 minutes or until all the water has fully absorbed. Fluff it up with a fork like you would rice or couscous once it's done.

2. Meanwhile, toss all the remaining ingredients together in a mixing bowl, coating everything well, before stirring through the quinoa until fully mixed together. Tweak the seasoning before serving and make any adjustments as you wish.

Why not try...

You can omit the Parma ham for a vegetarian version; it would also be lovely alongside some grilled chicken.

Barry's Tip

Please do wash the quinoa, it's pretty important to get the best flavour.

Pork TENDERLOIN SCHNITZEL

3 slices of bread, crusts removed

6 fresh sage leaves

1 tbsp grated Parmesan

seasoned flour (50g plain flour mixed with a good tbsp pepper and a pinch of salt)

1 egg, beaten

500g pork tenderloin, fat and sinew removed

knob of butter

4 tbsp olive oil

handful of fresh parsley

½ shallot

1 tsp capers

handful of fresh mint

1 tbsp red wine vinegar

To serve:

buttered new potatoes and green beans

Barry's Tip

Resting the meat is super-important, as it gives the juices a chance to get back to their roots and not just spill out when you slice the meat open. If you don't rest the meat, all that juice you see on the chopping board is wasted. It's flavour and you want that in your belly, not in the washing-up bowl.

I have absolutely fallen in love with these juicy strips of meat! This awesome loin gets crusted in a sage and Parmesan breadcrumb, pan-fried until golden and then baked until juicy. Served with a zingy caper and mint dressing, it's great with some buttered new potatoes and green beans.

1. Preheat the oven to 200°C/180°C fan/400°F/Gas mark 6.

2. Make some fresh breadcrumbs. Blitz the bread, sage and Parmesan in a food processor until fine and well mixed, then put in a shallow dish. Place the seasoned flour on a large plate and the egg in another shallow dish.

3. Dip the tenderloin first in the flour, then in the egg and then in the breadcrumbs until it's coated all over.

4. Put the butter and 1 tablespoon of olive oil in a frying pan, and let the pan warm up. Once the butter is bubbling, carefully add the tenderloin (cut it in half if it's too big for your pan) and cook for a good 5 minutes on each side until it's a lovely golden colour. Once all the sides are done, place on a baking tray and bake on the middle shelf of the oven for a good 15–18 minutes, depending on the thickness of your pork. Remove from the oven and leave to rest.

5. Meanwhile, make a zingy sauce. In a blender, whizz the parsley, shallot, capers and mint until finely chopped. Transfer to a little pot and mix in the remaining olive oil and the vinegar. You can tweak these flavour combos if you find them a little intense.

6. Slice the juicy tenderloin into thin discs (don't freak out if it's pale pink in some patches, that's fine) and serve the tangy sauce spooned over the pork alongside some buttered new potatoes and green beans for a flavour-packed dinner.

Why not try...

Keeping hold of some of the tenderloin and having it for lunch the next day as part of a salad or in a sandwich? It's just as delicious cold.

Toad
TARTE
TATIN

1 tsp olive oil

5 pork sausages (flavoured ones like pork and tomato, etc. work well)

6 shallots, peeled and sliced

2 tbsp red wine vinegar

1 heaped tbsp brown sugar

5 cherry tomatoes, halved

butter, for greasing

handful of fresh thyme, leaves only

230g pack ready-rolled all-butter puff pastry, rolled out slightly larger than your flan dish

salt and pepper

few cubes of goat's cheese (optional)

fresh basil leaves, to garnish

To serve:

salad

This is a little idea I had; I really wanted to put a toad in the hole recipe in here but thought I'd put a little tweak on it by merging it with the concept of a tarte tatin. Here, caramelised shallots, sausages and tomatoes are flipped out into a lovely little tarte o' loving that you'll go crazy for!

1. Preheat the oven to 200°C/180°C fan/400°F/Gas mark 6. Heat the olive oil in a frying pan over a medium heat and fry the sausages, until browned all over. Once done, set them aside on a plate and halve lengthways when they are cool enough to handle.

2. Put the shallots into the pan and, using the oil leftover from the sausages, cook for about 4–5 minutes until softened.

3. Pour the vinegar and sugar into the frying pan, reduce the heat to low and let bubble gently, stirring, for another 2 minutes. Add the tomato halves for the last couple of minutes to slightly soften them. Take off the heat.

4. In a buttered 24cm flan dish, arrange the sausages cut-side facing up, tomatoes cut-side down (get that?!), then spoon the shallot vinegar mixture all over the tomatoes and sausages, filling in the gaps. Try to fill it evenly all the way round, leaving a little gap between it and the side of the dish. Sprinkle with the thyme leaves, then cut the pastry into a rough circle shape, slightly larger than the dish, and drape it over the sausage mixture, tucking the edges down the side. Pierce a few holes with a fork and bake in the oven for 20–25 minutes until the base has risen and is lightly golden brown.

5. Take out of the oven and – this is the tricky/exciting/scary bit – sit a plate on top of the flan, then, using oven gloves, flip the tarte carefully and swiftly upside down onto the plate (give it a few seaside taps like a sandcastle). Remove the flan dish and – hey presto – you've got a bubbling, caramelised tarte tatin in the hole. Scatter the goat's cheese over the top, if you like, garnish with basil leaves and serve with salad.

Why not try...

Making a vegetarian version? Omit the sausages and caramelise a load of mixed vegetables together – in fact, I'm off to make one now!

Barry's Tip

I've made this three times as I write this and each time I flip it I feel it's not gonna come out of the flan dish, but it has every time. I'm doing it while it's hot, which I think helps, but if on the off-chance yours doesn't fall out, don't worry. It will still taste great – honest!

1.6–1.8kg pork shoulder, fat removed

50ml water

2 tbsp olive oil mixed with 1 tsp smoked paprika

8 ciabatta rolls, warmed

Rub:

1 heaped tsp cayenne pepper

1 heaped tsp onion powder

1 heaped tsp garlic powder

1 tsp pepper

pinch of mild chilli powder

3 tbsp smoked paprika

2 tsp dried mustard powder

1 tbsp light brown sugar

1 tbsp ground cumin

BBQ Sauce:

100ml ketchup

60ml rice wine vinegar

20ml cider vinegar

1 tbsp wholegrain mustard

¼ onion, peeled and diced

1 tsp Worcestershire sauce

2 tbsp runny honey

pinch of ground cinnamon

2 tsp soy sauce

1 tbsp apple juice

To serve:

Rainbow coleslaw (see page 220)

Avocado Salsa (see page 220)

There are some things I've made that have just completely blown my socks off and this is without doubt one of them; slow-cooked pulled pork drenched in a homemade barbecue sauce. It's all customisable so you can tweak it to be as tangy (or untangy) as you like. Get some good ciabattas to serve them in to soak up some of the sauce and you'll be in heaven.

1. Preheat the oven to 140°C/120°C fan/275°F/Gas mark 1.

2. Put all the rub ingredients into a small bowl and mix together with a spoon. Sit the pork in a large roasting tin and rub the mixture in, working into the nooks and crannies as much as possible. Cook, uncovered, on the middle shelf in the oven for an hour, just letting the heat do its thing.

3. Take the pork out of the oven, pour the water into the bottom of the tray then, using a pastry brush, coat the pork all over with the oil and paprika mixture. Cover with foil and return to the oven for a further 5½ hours, basting halfway through with the oily juices. Once the pork is cooked, set aside to rest.

4. Make the BBQ sauce. Combine all the ingredients in a large saucepan and cook over a medium heat until thickened, about 15 minutes.

5. Meanwhile, using two forks like cat claws, shred the pork on a chopping board – it should come apart easily – then literally dump the meat into the lightly bubbling BBQ sauce, stirring and coating it completely. This is a lovely thing.

6. Serve the pork loaded into your ciabattas. They are great warmed in the oven, then halved and topped with a good helping of coleslaw and salsa. You could put some Sweet Potato Wedges in the oven towards the end of the cooking time (see page 223) too.

Why not try...
Using any pork leftovers to make some nachos or fajitas?

BBQ *Pulled Pork* CIABATTAS

250g watermelon, deseeded and diced

250g honeydew melon, deseeded and diced

150g strawberries, hulled and halved

½ red onion, peeled and sliced

2 tbsp extra virgin olive oil

1 tbsp acacia honey

zest and juice of 1 lemon

zest and juice of ½ lime

100g spinach leaves

50g watercress

good handful of fresh mint, chopped

8–10 slices prosciutto

balsamic dressing, to finish

salt and pepper

Parmesan cheese shavings, to serve

Sometimes the simplest things are the best and this salad just works on so many levels, plus it looks pretty appealing too. It's light, delicious and uses a real variety of flavours – the freshness of the strawberries and melon, the zing of the citrus fruit and the silky saltiness of the prosciutto, to name a few. It's the sort of salad you could keep eating and not really get full on, but it makes you feel good. I love it and hope you do too!

1. Put the melons, strawberries and onion in a large bowl. Whisk together the olive oil, honey and the zest and juice of the lemon and lime. Season well and pour over the fruit to coat.

2. Combine the spinach, watercress and mint and put into individual bowls or onto a large board/platter. Top with the flavoured onion and fruit mixture, arrange the prosciutto over the top, then finish with a few shakes of balsamic dressing, some seasoning and Parmesan shavings.

Why not try...

Making the salad a little more lively by scattering over some deseeded chopped chillies or adding some mustard to the honey, oil and citrus fruits?

Barry's Tip
It's a relatively sweet salad so give the balsamic dressing a really good shake before using if you want to tone it down a bit.

Prosciutto, STRAWBERRY & MELON SALAD

Bacon
RIGATONI
CARBONARA

2 large egg yolks

25g Parmesan, grated, plus extra for sprinkling

40ml low-fat crème fraîche

200g rigatoni

1 tbsp olive oil

4 rashers unsmoked bacon, fat removed, cut into thin strips

4 spring onions, sliced

1 garlic clove, chopped

salt and pepper

1 tbsp chopped fresh parsley

To serve:

Garlic Bread (see page 229)

Carbonara is one of my most favourite things to make, I just love it. One day I hope to go to Italy and taste an authentic one for myself, but for now a decent homemade version really hits the spot. It's quick, filling, with just the right balance of flavours and you tend to have most of the ingredients around the kitchen to throw it together.

1. Whisk the egg yolks, Parmesan and crème fraîche together in a bowl, season a little and set aside for a moment.

2. Cook the rigatoni in a saucepan of boiling water until "al dente", according to the packet instructions. Drain, reserving 2–3 tablespoons of the cooking water.

3. Meanwhile, heat the oil in a frying pan over a medium flame and cook the bacon for 2–3 minutes. Add the spring onions and cook for another couple of minutes until the bacon is golden and the spring onions are softened. Add the garlic for a minute to soften up, then turn the heat to low and pour in the pasta, stirring gently to warm through for 1–2 minutes.

4. Finally, remove the pan from the heat and pour the egg mixture over the pasta and bacon, stirring for a minute or two so that it coats but doesn't scramble. Don't overdo it; use the pasta water to help thin out the egg. Season and serve immediately with a sprinkling of parsley and extra Parmesan. Serve with some garlic bread alongside.

Why not try...
Load up the carbonara with chunks of chicken, mushrooms and peas.

Barry's Tip
If you can't get rigatoni use whatever pasta you have – penne, spaghetti and fettucine all work great. The most important thing is to focus on the egg/cream mixture not scrambling; it's all about working fast and controlling the heat.

Parma Ham,
ARTICHOKE & ASPARAGUS TART

Difficulty ●
Ready in **30 MINUTES**
Serves **4**

This super-speedy tart is a great no-fuss recipe to rustle up in a hurry; it's got a lovely tangy pesto vibe running through it balanced with the textures of Parma ham, asparagus and artichoke. Topping with fresh mint and Parmesan just completes the dish and will hit the spot if you need a quick fix. Super customisable, try it like this then tweak it your way.

small pack ready-rolled puff pastry

3 tbsp green pesto

8 thin asparagus spears

small jar artichoke chunks, drained

6 strips of Parma ham

1 egg, beaten

roughly 4 tbsp frozen peas, thawed

fresh mint leaves, picked

handful of Parmesan shavings

To serve:

salad

1. Preheat the oven to 190°C/170°C fan/375°F/Gas mark 5. Roll out the puff pastry to approximately 30 x 22cm so it fits snuggly into a baking tray, then cut away any excess. With a knife, lightly score a border around the edge of the pastry about 2½cm all the way round.

2. Spoon on the pesto, smearing it evenly over the pastry up to the borderline.

3. Top the pesto base with the asparagus, artichokes and Parma ham – make it look as flashy as you like! Brush the untouched border with beaten egg and bake in the oven for 10 minutes before adding the peas. Return to the oven and bake for a further 5 minutes or so until the pastry is golden brown and risen.

4. Remove from the oven, sprinkle over the mint and the Parmesan shavings. Serve up with a side salad of your choice.

Why not try...

There is no end to what you can do here – red pesto with a load of vegetables and tomatoes with a sort-of Mediterranean vibe would be really good.

Barry's Tip

You can make this without a border if you prefer, taking the ingredients all the way out to the edges, almost like a pastry flatbread.

FISH
&
SEAFOOD

ROAST COD PAELLA WITH CHORIZO & PEAS
MIXED FISH 'CHOWDA' BREAD BOWLS
PRAWN & HALLOUMI WITH A WATERMELON SALAD
FINGER LICKIN' FISH FINGER BAPS
ZESTY MACKEREL NOODLES
LITTLE FISHY IN A LITTLE DISHY
PANCETTA-WRAPPED POLLOCK TRAYBAKE
BABY CRAB CAKE BITES WITH REMOULADE DIP
YUMMY YUMMY SALMON TERIYAKI FINGERS
SEA BASS & PRAWN KEDGEREE
PEPPERED SALMON & ASPARAGUS ONE-POT PASTA
CAJUN FISH TACO
SESAME-CRUSTED TUNA
BEER-BATTERED FISH & CHIPS

200g basmati rice

600ml chicken stock, made with 1 cube

pinch of saffron

1 tbsp olive oil

1 red onion, peeled and diced

½ red pepper, deseeded and chopped into squares

150g chorizo, sliced into small pieces

1 tsp turmeric (optional)

1 tsp paprika (optional)

280g skinless cod fillets, cut into chunks

handful of frozen peas

salt and pepper

To serve:

crusty bread and butter

Barry's Tip

Please be careful when transferring the rice mixture to the casserole dish. Push gently with a spoon making sure that the rice goes into the dish first, then slowly drizzle the stock from the pan into the dish (don't wear flip flops like I do as it'll burn even if a little splodge hits your foot...trust me!).

I love this recipe, it's great on a budget and, like other recipes cooked in a casserole dish, it is full of flavour. Basmati rice is cooked with stock and saffron (oooh, flashy!) and chucked in a casserole with chorizo, peas, onions, peppers and cod – it's simple, can be tweaked so much and it works!

1. Preheat the oven to 190°C/170°C fan/375°F/Gas mark 5.

2. Wash the rice by putting it in a ovenproof dish, adding water and gently stirring with your fingertips. The water should go murky, then drain – not through a sieve, you don't want to damage the rice – but through your hand and repeat until the water runs clear.

3. Add the saffron to the stock and leave the flavours to infuse.

4. Heat the olive oil in a frying pan over a medium heat, add the onion, red pepper and chorizo and fry for 3–4 minutes. Add the rice and stir-fry for 90 seconds, making sure the rice is coated in all the pan oils.

5. Pour in the chicken stock and bring to the boil. Once it's boiling, carefully pour the contents into an ovenproof dish, cover with a lid and cook on the middle shelf for 15 minutes. Keep your eye on the water level and top up with more water if necessary.

6. Meanwhile, rub the turmeric and paprika over the fish chunks, if you like – this adds greater colour and flavour to the fish, but Mrs Barry prefers it milder so I tend to skip this step.

7. Remove the dish from the oven and stir to check the consistency. Top up the water if necessary. Stir in the peas, place the fish on top and season generously. Cover again and bake for 10 more minutes until the fish is cooked through.

8. Once ready, either serve on a plate with the cooked fish on top or, if you want to be a bit rustic, use a fork to flake the fish and stir it through the rice. Whatever you do, serve with crusty bread and butter!

Why not try...

Making this a good few hours ahead, then reheating until piping hot all the way through, ready for dinner when you get home? Like a chilli, when reheated this dish becomes even more flavoursome.

Roast Cod Paella
WITH CHORIZO & PEAS

Mixed Fish 'CHOWDA' BREAD BOWLS

Difficulty ●
Ready in 40 MINUTES
Serves 8

8 freshly baked medium crusty bread bowls

750ml water

2 fish or chicken stock cubes

1 carrot, peeled and chopped into small chunks

500g potatoes, peeled and chopped into cubes

1 celery stick, chopped into small chunks

600g mixed fish, e.g. smoked haddock, salmon, white fish, prawns (if you're feeling posh), cut into 2cm cubes

50g butter, melted and left at room temperature

2 good handfuls of fresh parsley, chopped

salt and pepper

320g tin sweetcorn, drained

100g cubed pancetta or smoked streaky bacon, diced (optional)

a little oil, for cooking

200ml low-fat double cream

handful of fresh chives

knob of butter, melted

This is another dish that brings back some great memories of my time spent in Boston, USA – chowder, or, as the locals pronounce it, 'chowda' (there's a funny *Simpsons* sketch which summarises this well!). It is essentially a creamy, thick, brothy, soup social-club of fish fun that is just so right – any time of year. I'm combining this with another experience my adopted American mom and sister Cindy and Samantha introduced me to – bread bowls. So good. Tweak this how you like, play around with it, just love it and it'll love you back. You may struggle to find a good-sized bread bowl; if that's the case the chowder on its own is perfectly good for just dunking in a slice of bread.

1. Prepare the bread bowls. Slice off lids from the bread and pick out the insides leaving a good 1cm wall, plus the crust, of course! Set aside the hollowed-out bread for serving.

2. Bring the water to the boil in a large saucepan. Stir in the stock cubes, then add the carrot, potatoes and celery and cook for 10–15 minutes until the vegetables start to soften and become tender. Allow to cool for 5 minutes.

3. Meanwhile, put the fish into a sealable bag, pour in the melted butter, throw in a handful of chopped parsley and some salt and pepper, then close the bag and shake it around until evenly covered.

4. Next, whizz the veg mixture in a blender, and pour it back into the saucepan. Add the sweetcorn and heat for about 8–10 minutes.

5. Meanwhile, fry the cubed pancetta or bacon (if using) in a small frying pan with a drop of oil until lightly browned. Drain on kitchen paper.

6. Put the fish mixture and cream into the pan with the veg, stir, lower the heat, keeping it just beneath a simmer, and cook for about 5 minutes until the fish is cooked. For the final minute stir through the rest of the parsley and the chives, and season to taste.

7. Pour the chowder into the bread bowls (if using) or individual bowls, top with the bacon (if using) and herbs and season if needed. Dunk in the hollowed-out bread, eat the chowder, then eat the bowl!

Prawn & Halloumi WITH A WATERMELON SALAD

150g halloumi cheese, cut thinly into 6 slices/squares

150g raw king prawns, deveined

1 tsp olive oil

250g watermelon, deseeded and cubed

5 tsp red wine vinegar

2 tsp sugar

2 tbsp finely chopped fresh mint

½ small red onion, peeled and finely sliced

70g rocket leaves

100g frozen broad beans, thawed and podded

1 lemon

Originally this recipe was going to be skewered, but I had a fiddly job trying to get all the halloumi on without it splitting, and I don't want you guys wasting any. In this recipe prawns and halloumi are griddled and served over a watermelon salad with onions, broad beans and a lovely watermelon dressing – it's light, quick and refreshing.

1. Warm a griddle pan to piping hot. Brush the cheese and prawns with the olive oil and cook in the pan for 2 minutes on each side.

2. Meanwhile, make the dressing by whizzing together half your watermelon with the vinegar and sugar in a blender.

3. In a mixing bowl, toss the mint, onion, rocket, broad beans and the zest from your lemon together until well combined. Pour in a little of the melon dressing.

4. Stack the salad on a serving plate with the halloumi, prawns and remaining melon cubes staggered over the top. Drizzle over the remaining melon dressing and squeeze the juice from the lemon over the top.

Why not try...
This recipe on the BBQ (weather permitting, of course)!

Barry's Tip
I recommend doubling up the amount of dressing to give you a little extra for drizzling over the prawns and halloumi just before serving, for an added melon top-up.

4 tbsp light mayonnaise

1 tbsp fresh mint

1 tbsp capers

pepper

zest and juice of 1 lemon

small bowl ready-made breadcrumbs

2 frozen cod steaks (roughly 350g), thawed, drained of excess water

small bowl plain flour

1 egg, beaten

1 tbsp olive oil

2 large finger baps/Vienna rolls/large hot-dog rolls

4 tbsp ketchup (or as you need!)

¼ lettuce, washed and roughly chopped (use red lettuce if you have it)

What is not to love about fish finger sandwiches? Nothing really, except I'd kinda like them a little fatter and write a recipe for that – oh, hang on...this is my recipe book so I'm gonna do just that! This is a super yummy, cheap, quick fix that'll become your legendary go-to on a Sunday evening, you know, when you're a little peckish and you're not sure what to eat? Get this in your arsenal and you'll be hopping on a pogo stick of taste-bud satisfaction.

1. Preheat the oven to 190°C/170°C fan/375°F/Gas mark 5.

2. Whizz together the mayo, mint, capers, a pinch of pepper and of lemon zest and a short squeeze of lemon juice. Dip your finger in and have a taste, tweak to your liking, then set aside.

3. Sprinkle the remaining lemon zest and a pinch of pepper into the breadcrumbs and mix gently with your fingers. Dunk the fish in flour, then the egg, then the breadcrumbs, coating fully and evenly all over. Dip them back in again if there are patches until you have a lovely looking, uncooked, breaded fish beast.

4. Heat the olive oil in a frying pan over a medium heat, then once hot brown the fish on all its sides (a couple of minutes each side, edges too if you can) before transferring to a baking tray and cooking in the oven for around 15 minutes.

5. Warm the buns in the microwave for 10 seconds, slice in half, spread the base with a little mint mayo and ketchup, add a good handful of lettuce, add in the breaded fish pieces, drizzle more minty mayo on top, extra lettuce, then a good squirt of ketchup, before placing the lid on top. Squirt some lemon juice over if you feel like it.

6. Take a picture and hashtag it #myvirginkitchen on your social media network of choice, then eat away.

Why not try...

You can whack them in the oven for 20 minutes from the start if you prefer, but I've found the colour doesn't come out so good; of course, this depends on the breadcrumbs used too.

Barry's Tip
If you have any leftover bread you can whizz it up to make fresh breadcrumbs.

Finger Lickin'
FISH FINGER BAPS

Zesty
**MACKEREL
NOODLES**

90ml olive oil, plus 1 tsp
for the peppers

zest and juice of 1 orange

1 tbsp honey

1 mango, peeled, stoned
and roughly chopped

1 red chilli, deseeded and
roughly chopped

1 yellow pepper, deseeded
and cut into strips

4 raw smoked mackerel
(about 250g)

150g fresh rice noodles

75g watercress, woody
stems removed

1 tub cress, washed and
snipped from the soil

15g fresh mint, roughly
chopped

pepper

6 slices of chorizo

This is just a recipe I chucked together when Mrs Barry was on the way back from an exercise class and was 'starving'. So with a few random ingredients around the house I came up with this little stonker. A few years back I would have just ordered a pizza, but it's one of Mrs Barry's favourite things now so it had to be in here. Hope you give it a go and put your own twist on it.

1. Pour the olive oil, half the orange juice and the honey into a bowl. Don't stir it yet, just put it to one side (please).

2. In a blender, whizz the mango chunks and chilli to a pulp. Pour this into the oily orange mixture and stir well to thoroughly combine.

3. Heat a griddle pan over a medium heat. Coat the yellow pepper in 1 teaspoon of olive oil and, when hot, lay them on the griddle to blister, roughly 3–4 minutes on each side, then put them on a plate.

4. Cook the fish on the griddle for about 2–3 minutes on each side, giving them a squeeze of orange juice as they cook, then turn off the heat and set aside.

5. Meanwhile, heat a frying pan and warm the rice noodles for about 2 minutes, lightly stirring to break up any tangles.

6. Put the watercress, cress and mint into a large bowl, add the warm noodles, 1 tablespoon of the mango dressing, then toss everything together to coat. Season with pepper and add a little orange zest.

7. Place the chorizo slices into the rice-noodle pan with the peppers (just to warm them) and cook for 90 seconds or so until the chorizo starts to crease and release a little oil.

8. Serve on a plate with a good handful of the noodle/cress mixture, put the chorizo slices on top, then the fish, overlapping each other – squeeze over more orange juice, add some charred peppers and drizzle the remaining mango dressing over and around the plate.

Why not try...
Flaking the fish with a fork and mixing it all together as one big zesty noodle pile?

Barry's Tip
You can, of course, do this all in one pan; I just like the griddle lines on the peppers/fish.

Little fishy
IN A LITTLE DISHY

2 knobs of butter

1 onion, peeled and sliced

1 yellow pepper, deseeded and cut into small dice

50g runner beans, trimmed and cut into small pieces

1 tsp plain flour

1 tsp mustard powder

Please excuse the name but this is such a great little dish(y), that my kids absolutely adore eating – individual tuna fish pies with their very own cheesy, sweet potato, rosti topping. They are speedy to throw together, and packed full of good stuff that you can tweak too. Make a larger fishy in a larger dishy for a more grown-up version!

1. In a frying pan over a medium heat, melt a knob of butter until bubbling, then tip in the onion, yellow pepper and runner beans and cook, stirring occasionally, for a good 4–5 minutes to soften.

1 courgette, cut into small dice

good handful of fresh curly leaf parsley, chopped

410g tin evaporated milk

1 vegetable stock cube

pepper

300g tinned tuna in spring water, drained

150g sweet potato, peeled and halved

100g Cheddar cheese, grated

broccoli, to serve

2. Next, add the flour and mustard powder, stirring to combine, then add the courgette, parsley and evaporated milk. Crumble in the stock cube, stir thoroughly and simmer for a good 5 minutes. Season with pepper and tip in the tinned tuna to warm through for 2 minutes, breaking the fish down into smaller pieces.

3. Meanwhile, cook the sweet potato in a pan of boiling water for 5–7 minutes or until almost tender but still firm enough to coarsely grate. Drain and refresh under cold water. Melt the other knob of butter in a pan, grate the potato and add to the melted butter, stirring gently to combine. Season with pepper.

4. When the tuna mixture is warmed through, preheat the grill. Spoon into individual ramekins or small pie dishes, then top with a mixture of the sweet potato and grated cheese and put under the grill for a good 5–7 minutes until golden brown on top. Serve with some broccoli but eat straight out of the ramekins!

Why not try...
Mixing up the fish used here or switching it up with cooked chicken chunks instead?

Pancetta-Wrapped POLLOCK TRAYBAKE

Difficulty ●
Ready in **25 MINUTES**
Serves **2**

about 20 red and yellow cherry tomatoes, halved

1 courgette, thinly sliced

4 asparagus spears, snipped into small sections

handful of fresh thyme

2 tsp dried oregano

1½ tbsp red wine vinegar

300g pollock, skinned and cut into little chunks

small pack of pancetta strips

olive oil, for drizzling

Barry's Tip
If you can't get pollock, use haddock, hake or cod instead.

There's something about this traybake that blows my mind, it's so simple to prepare and cook, yet it's full of flavour. It also looks pretty cool with the herbs scattered over the mixed coloured tomatoes and wrapped fish. All in all, it won't let you down and is great to make in a hurry.

1. Preheat the oven to 180°C/160°C fan/350°F/Gas mark 4.

2. Arrange the tomatoes, courgette and asparagus in a baking tray, then scatter over the thyme and 1 teaspoon of oregano. Drizzle over the vinegar, then bake in the oven for 10 minutes to soften the vegetables.

3. Meanwhile, wrap the cubes of fish in the strips of pancetta, putting them join-side down on a board to stop them unravelling.

4. When the vegetables are done, put the wrapped fish in the tray and sprinkle over the remaining teaspoon of dried oregano. Drizzle with the olive oil. Bake for a good 10–12 minutes until the pancetta is lightly browned.

Why not try...
Believe it or not, this is actually really good cold. The sweetness of the dish is quite nice to nibble on as a little snack.

Fish & Seafood

Baby Crab Cake Bites
WITH REMOULADE DIP

50g breadcrumbs

2 tbsp chopped fresh coriander

1 tsp smoked paprika

salt and pepper

handful of spring onions, finely chopped

250g fresh white crabmeat

½ red chilli, deseeded and finely chopped

zest and juice of 1 lemon, plus wedges to serve

1 tsp honey

1 medium egg yolk

plain flour, for coating

2 tbsp olive oil

For the cheat's remoulade:

100g mayonnaise

1 tbsp Dijon mustard

2 tbsp pickle relish

1 tsp cayenne pepper

1 tbsp hot cayenne sauce (most supermarkets stock this)

1 tbsp horseradish sauce

1 garlic clove, peeled and finely chopped

I really struggle to think of crab cakes and not think of a cake made of crab… Just me? Okay then. These baby crab cakes are deliciously simple to bring together and they've got a lovely citrus and coriander vibe going on. Crab isn't a headline act in the Glastonbury of food, but it's great and definitely gives tuna a run for its money. We are serving it here with a kicking, speedy, remoulade-style dip which you can tweak to your liking or perhaps dunk in a sweet chilli sauce instead – all good!

1. Make the remoulade first by combining all the ingredients together in a bowl, adjusting to taste (the cayenne and horseradish have a good kick so maybe add them gradually), then chill in the fridge.

2. In a mixing bowl, combine the breadcrumbs, coriander, paprika, pinch of salt and pepper, spring onions, crabmeat, chilli, lemon juice and zest and honey, adding just a little beaten egg at a time until it comes together and is super-combined.

3. Spread the flour on a plate. Roll the crab mixture into 12–14 small balls, then roll each in the flour to lightly coat. Flatten down slightly to form a disc, then place on a chopping board and chill in the fridge for 10–15 minutes to help them hold their shape.

4. Heat the olive oil (it should be enough to cover the base of the pan completely but only just) in a frying pan over a medium heat. When hot, cook the cakes on both sides for 2–3 minutes until browned – do this in batches if you prefer, putting them on kitchen paper until they are all done.

5. Serve the cakes with the remoulade dip, lemon wedges and a couple of items from the pick 'n' mix section (see pages 220–229) – a handful of rocket with some chargrilled vegetables would work a charm too!

Why not try…
Warming up some pitta breads and filling them with salad, mayo, remoulade and the crab cakes for a punchy hands-on bite?

Yummy Yummy SALMON TERIYAKI FINGERS

1 garlic clove, peeled and finely chopped

70g caster sugar

60ml white wine

60ml soy sauce

4 skinless salmon fillets

10 asparagus spears, washed, woody ends removed

2 tbsp vegetable oil

4 spring onions, sliced

2 tsp sesame seeds, plus extra to serve

400g fresh egg noodles

My first discovery of teriyaki came when I was travelling in America with Mrs Barry. We were at a train station in Chicago and there was a stall selling teriyaki salmon and the lady was shouting 'yummy yummy' over and over. Eventually we gave in and tried it, and I'll never forget the taste. In this recipe I've tried to replicate it by making a super-speedy teriyaki noodle dish, which Mrs Barry says is also 'yummy yummy'. Make the marinade ahead and you'll have this on the table in a flash.

1. Combine the garlic, sugar, wine and soy sauce in a bowl, stirring until the sugar has dissolved. Taste and tweak to your liking, then put the mixture into a sealable bag. Put the salmon in the bag, seal and give it a gentle shake to coat it, then marinate in the fridge for at least 20 minutes, but the longer the better.

2. When you are ready to cook, cut the asparagus into quarters on a diagonal angle. Heat a wok nice and hot with 1 tablespoon vegetable oil. Add the asparagus and spring onions and cook for 5 minutes to soften.

3. Meanwhile, heat the remaining oil in a frying pan over a medium heat. When hot, add the salmon, leaving as much marinade as possible in the bag and cook for 3–4 minutes on each side until golden brown.

4. Pour the leftover marinade and sesame seeds into the wok with the vegetables – it may make a little sizzle at first but it's all good. Stir-fry for a further minute to coat the vegetables.

5. Add the noodles to the pan and warm through according to the package instructions. Fresh noodles won't take long, about 2–3 minutes. While it's warming, using a spatula, work the marinade, asparagus and spring onions through it.

6. Serve the noodles, topped with the golden salmon and some of the leftover marinade poured over the top. Add a sprinkle of sesame seeds to finish.

Why not try...

Using the marinade with different meats, like chicken or beef – it's very adaptable!

Barry's Tip
Keep your eye on the salmon when cooking/ flipping, it will become delicate as it softens, so turn it carefully.

Sea Bass & Prawn KEDGEREE

6 eggs

300g basmati rice

2 knobs of butter, plus extra at room temperature, to serve

250ml water

500ml vegetable stock

1 onion, peeled and a small wedge cut out, the rest diced

handful of black peppercorns

1 bay leaf

300g sea bass fillets, skin removed

1 tbsp chopped fresh parsley

150g raw king prawns

1 heaped tbsp mild curry powder

2 cardamom pods bashed, seeds only

1 green chilli, deseeded and finely chopped

1 lemon, cut into thin wedges

salt and pepper

good handful of chopped fresh coriander

I have never tried making kedgeree before writing this book, but had always wanted to give it a go. Apparently back in Victorian times it was considered a breakfast dish, but you can eat this any time of day – it's great! This version is a subtly spiced kedgeree with prawns and poached sea bass, but you can increase the strength to your liking. I guarantee it will be a hit.

1. Put the eggs into a saucepan of water and bring to the boil, then lower the heat and simmer for 8–10 minutes. Plunge the eggs into cold water, then peel off the shells and set aside.

2. Meanwhile, put the rice in a bowl, add enough water to cover and gently stir with your fingertips. The water should go murky, then drain – not through a sieve, you don't want to damage the rice – through your hand and repeat until the water runs clear. Put the rice into a pan with a knob of butter and the 250ml water, stir, then cover with a lid and bring to the boil. Once boiling point is reached, turn down the heat to low and simmer for 15 minutes.

3. Bring the vegetable stock, onion wedge, peppercorns and bay leaf to a simmer in another pan, add the fish and poach for 4–5 minutes, then set aside. Keep a few tablespoons of the stock for later.

4. Heat another knob of butter and the parsley in another pan, then add the prawns and fry for 3–4 minutes. Set the prawns aside, then add the diced onion, curry powder, cardamom seeds and chilli to the pan and fry for 5 minutes until the onion is soft.

5. Tip the onion mixture, sea bass and prawns into the rice and stir gently to flake the fish a little. Spoon in the reserved stock, give a squirt of lemon juice from one of the wedges, a good season and a little more butter and stir again.

6. Cut the reserved eggs into quarters, then add to the rice with the remaining lemon wedges before topping with a good handful of chopped coriander and serving.

Why not try...
Ramping the strength up a little? Use smoked haddock as it has a stronger flavour.

Peppered Salmon & ASPARAGUS ONE-POT PASTA

300g pasta

8 asparagus spears

150ml water

1 vegetable stock cube

150g smoked salmon, sliced into little squares

pepper

150ml double cream

small bunch of chopped fresh coriander, plus extra to serve

2 tsp grated Parmesan cheese, plus extra for coating

Barry's Tip

When mixing the pasta through, try not to use a wooden spoon. A spatula has become my friend a lot in my journey – it's more delicate and will hopefully not break up your pasta. This works for other things like rice, too, so remember – a spatula is your friend!

Nothing is better than a one-pot dish, and a one-pot dish that actually tastes amazing at that – trust me, there are some shockers out there! This is delicious in every way; a lovely creamy sauce, great velvety pasta, combined with yummy peppered salmon and asparagus chunks.

1. Boil the kettle, then fill the saucepan two-thirds of the way up with the boiling water, add the pasta and cook according to the packet instructions.

2. Meanwhile, snip off the tough stalks on the asparagus with scissors, then wash and slice the spears into thirds.

3. A couple of minutes before the pasta is done, drop the asparagus into the pan and cook for 2–3 minutes. Drain, reserving a small amount of the cooking water.

4. In the same saucepan, pour in the 150ml water, then crumble in the stock cube and stir over a low heat. Season the salmon well with pepper.

5. Pour the cream into the pan with the chopped coriander and the salmon, then stir to combine well and warm to just below boiling point.

6. Remove the pan from the heat and let the pasta and asparagus join in the one-pot loving. Mix the pasta in well until it is covered in the sauce, adding the Parmesan as you go.

7. Plonk a good helping on a plate, spoon some extra sauce from the pan on top, if you wish, then top with extra chopped coriander, Parmesan and pepper to your liking. So good!

Why not try...

Different fish or vegetable combos? Lesser-used fish such as tilapia could work really well here, or if you have a lot of cauliflower or broccoli use that instead of the asparagus – or add it as well, giving it even more depth and texture.

Cajun
FISH
TACO

1 tbsp salt

1 tbsp dried oregano

1 tbsp cayenne pepper

1 tbsp onion granules

1 tbsp smoked paprika, plus an extra pinch for the mayo

100g mayonnaise

1 lemon

2 tbsp sour cream

20g fresh coriander, chopped, plus extra to garnish

1 tsp English mustard

salt and pepper

4 pineapple rings, drained and cut into small chunks

100g cherry tomatoes, halved

1 large avocado, peeled, stoned and cut into small cubes

1 garlic clove, peeled and finely chopped

1 tbsp olive oil

3 large cod, haddock or coley fillets, skinned and boned

4 tortillas

This is quite a special recipe to me; not only does it literally blow my socks off but it's also the first recipe I ever cooked live at a food festival. I've used coley here, which is a great, sustainable, inexpensive fish which most supermarkets stock. I hope you love this as much as I do – super-tangy, kicking-fresh fish-loving in the palm of your hand.

1. Make the rub by putting the salt, oregano, cayenne pepper, onion granules and paprika into a sealable bag, sealing and shaking it until it looks like a lovely fake tan colour. Set aside.

2. Make the zingy mayonnaise by combining the mayo with the zest of half the lemon, 1 tablespoon of lemon juice, the sour cream, one-third of the coriander, the mustard, pepper and a pinch of paprika. Chill in the fridge.

3. In a bowl, combine the pineapple chunks, tomatoes, avocado, garlic, the remaining lemon juice and coriander, salt and pepper and toss well. Put in the fridge with the mayonnaise.

4. Put the oil into a frying pan and get it nice and hot. Meanwhile, put the fish on a chopping board and rub with the spice mix on both sides, staining it with colour and making sure it's well coated. Cook in the hot pan for 3 minutes on each side until browned.

5. Put the fish on a board and roughly flake with a fork, then warm the tortillas in the pan for 30 seconds or so on each side until warmed through and they have absorbed some of the Cajun flavours.

6. Lay the wraps on a board, put a good line of the pineapple salsa down the middle, top with the fish and the mayonnaise, then sprinkle over more coriander and a squeeze of lemon. Garnish with any leftover lemon pieces sliced into thin wedges and munch away.

Why not try...
Of course I've used coley here, but you can use other fish instead: cod, haddock, etc. Mix it up!

Sesame-
CRUSTED TUNA

100ml rice vinegar

2 tsp honey

50g radish, thinly sliced

½ cucumber, deseeded and finely sliced

1 carrot, peeled and thinly sliced on the diagonal

2 tbsp hoisin sauce

juice of ½ orange

1 tsp soy sauce

1 tsp sesame oil

250g tuna steak

10g sesame seeds

10g black sesame seeds/ poppy seeds/onion seeds

wok oil, for cooking

good handful of fresh egg noodles or udon noodles

Barry's Tip
The tuna will cook pretty fast indeedy, so pay attention so you don't overdo it!

Well, this dish is a lush little number, and it looks impressive too, considering the amount of effort needed. In this recipe tuna steaks are fried in a sesame crust, then piled onto noodles and pickled vegetables and drizzed with an orange hoisin sauce. It's super-light and zingy with a lovely range of textures.

1. Put the rice vinegar and honey into a bowl, mix briefly, then dunk in the radish, cucumber and carrot and leave to pickle. Make sure the vegetables are coated in the mixture, stirring halfway through.

2. Mix the hoisin sauce, orange juice, soy sauce and sesame oil together in a bowl. Tweak the flavours to your liking before dipping the tuna in and coating it in the marinade.

3. Put all the sesame seeds in another bowl and coat the tuna steaks in them. (Set the leftover marinade aside.) Heat a drop of oil in a frying pan over a medium heat, add the tuna and fry for about 1½ minutes on each side for medium rare, but cook longer if you want it less pink. Once done, slice the tuna into thin strips.

4. Tip the egg noodles into the tuna pan and warm through over the heat for 2 minutes, breaking them up with a spatula. Pour in a little of the reserved marinade to wake them up, but make sure you leave some marinade for serving. If you are using udon noodles, these take a little longer to cook so start them before cooking the tuna.

5. Put the noodles on a serving plate, add a good pile of the pickled vegetables on top, then some slices of tuna staggered across and a little remaining marinade drizzled over the top – super-yummy.

Why not try...
Using pork tenderloin instead of the tuna? Pork will need to be baked so it will take longer, or perhaps use chicken? This recipe is very flexible and I'd love to see what you come up with.

Beer-Battered
FISH & CHIPS

220g self-raising flour, plus extra for coating

sea salt and pepper

330ml good-quality bitter or ale of your choice, chilled

400g good-quality potatoes (Desiree or Maris Piper are good), skin on, cut into even chunky chips

1–2 tbsp olive oil, for chips

vegetable oil, for frying

2 x 200g (ish) plump cod, haddock or coley fillets, skinned and bones removed

To serve:

lemon wedges

tartare sauce

Barry's Tip

If you don't want to parboil the chips, whack them in the oven drenched in oil and seasoning for a good 35–40 minutes.

Growing up by the seaside it's hard not to have a little admiration for fish and chips; I guess it's even more authentic with a clump of accidental windswept sand over it. Cod is extremely popular in batter, and although we can make it healthier baked in breadcrumbs, there's really nothing like making your own batter! I've used coley here – a slightly cheaper and sustainable alternative to cod.

1. Preheat the oven to 230°C/210°C fan/450°F/Gas mark 8. Make the batter by mixing the flour with a good pinch of salt and pepper. Add the beer in 3 or 4 batches, whisking as you go; don't worry if there are a couple of lumps, but don't overwhisk it. You will have some batter left over, but I think it's better to have too much to make dunking easier later. Put the batter in the fridge to keep cool until needed.

2. Soften the potatoes in a pan of boiling water for 4–5 minutes. Check with a knife to make sure they are soft but still a little firm. Drain and pat dry with kitchen paper, then tip into a bowl with the olive oil and season to your liking with salt and pepper.

3. Bake the chips in the oven for 18–20 minutes until golden brown. Halfway through baking, take them out of the oven and flip them over.

4. Put the vegetable oil in a deep-fat fryer and heat until the oil is a steady 180°C/350°F. You can also deep-fry in a large deep saucepan with a cooking thermometer, but be careful. The fish will take about 5 minutes to cook, so time this to finish with your chips. Cover the fillets in plain flour, then put them into the chilled batter to coat. Place the fish carefully in the oil and fry for 4–5 minutes until lightly golden. Fry the fillets separately if you prefer. Remove and pat with kitchen paper.

5. Serve the oven chips with extra salt and pepper to your liking, a piece of battered coley, some lemon wedges and tartare sauce.

Why not try...
Serving with minted peas, slightly mashed.

VEGGIE

GRIDDLED VEGETABLE BRUSCHETTA
MAC & CHEESE & PEAS
VEGGIE CON BEANIE
BROCCOLI PESTO SPAGHETTI
MY SEXY VIRGIN MARY SOUP
VEGETABLE & LENTIL CROWD-PLEASER
PUY LENTIL SALAD WITH ROAST BEETROOT
PEASY OVEN-BAKED RISOTTO
SPANISH (ISH) CRISP TORTILLA
FALAFEL HASH
SPICED SQUASH & COCONUT SOUP
WRAPATOUILLE
AUBERGINE & SPINACH MADRAS WARMER

Griddled VEGETABLE BRUSCHETTA

1 good-quality loaf (a nice wide pain de campagne or sourdough works well)

1 courgette, thinly sliced

1 yellow pepper, deseeded and sliced into small squares

16 cherry tomatoes, mixed colours if you like (based on around 4 tomatoes per bruschetta)

6 chestnut mushrooms, thickly sliced

extra-virgin olive oil

handful of grated mozzarella

chopped fresh basil

salt and pepper

Barry's Tip
You can remove the skins from the griddled tomatoes if you prefer – they'll just pull off with a pair of tongs.

Is it just me or is there something deliciously awesome about griddled vegetables? That amazing natural sweetness that they let out with a slight charred feel – yumtastic. In this recipe a medley of veg sits on toasted bread with basil and melted mozzarella – sometimes the simplest things are the best!

1. Heat a griddle pan over a medium-to-high heat until nice and hot. Slice the bread at diagonals into 10cm thick slices and either griddle on both sides until lightly charred or whack in the toaster until brown. Set aside.

2. Place the veg in the griddle pan and cook until completely softened. Try to get some light blister marks on the pepper and cherry tomatoes and get the courgettes and mushrooms nice and soft.

3. Preheat the grill to Medium. Drizzle the bread lightly with the olive oil, place about 4 cherry tomatoes on each slice of bread, squish down a little with a spoon to spread them out, if needed, then arrange the mushrooms, courgettes and peppers on top and sprinkle lightly with mozzarella.

4. Place under the grill to melt the cheese. Add a little extra oil if you like, then sprinkle with a little chopped basil and serve – so good!

Why not try...

Mixing it up with a tofu version? It may not sound appealing to all but if you can drive some flavour into it, say with some lemon, it works really well.

Mac & CHEESE & PEAS

250g macaroni

1 tbsp olive oil

1 onion, peeled and chopped

1 garlic clove, peeled and finely chopped

300ml light double cream

120g frozen peas

150ml water

1 vegetable stock cube (optional)

pepper

150g grated cheese (go for a mix of Cheddar and Red Leicester if you can, or pick one)

25g Parmesan, grated, plus extra for sprinkling (optional)

chopped fresh parsley, for sprinkling (optional)

I'm a bit of a late arrival to the mac and cheese love-in. As a child I never tried it; basically as it contained cheese I thought I would hate it! So some years later I gave it a go and indeed there are plenty of ways to make and pimp this classic, but this has always worked for me – a real cheap, filling, speedy crowd-pleaser.

1. Preheat the oven to 190°C/170°C fan/375°F/Gas mark 5.

2. Bring a saucepan of water to the boil, then tip in the macaroni and cook according to the packet instructions.

3. Meanwhile, heat the olive oil in a frying pan over a medium heat, add the onion and cook for a good 5 minutes to soften. Throw in the chopped garlic and cook for 2 more minutes.

4. Once the macaroni is cooked, drain it in a colander and set aside. Pour the cream into the pan with the onion, then add the peas, water and macaroni. Crumble over the stock cube, if using, and season with lots of pepper. Using a spatula, stir thoroughly over a low heat for 3 minutes or so just to warm through and to combine all the ingredients – don't boil it.

5. Take the pan off the heat and add the grated cheese, stirring and using the residual heat to melt the cheese. Pour the mixture into an ovenproof dish and scatter the Parmesan generously over the top. Bake on the middle shelf of the oven until golden brown on top – about 10–15 minutes, but keep your eye on it.

6. Spoon into bowls, top with some extra grated cheese, a sprinkling of chopped parsley and an extra sprinkling of pepper, if you like, then munch away.

Why not try...

Adding a bit of meat in there? Mac and cheese and gammon doesn't rhyme unfortunately, but it would work a charm.

Barry's Tip
The cheese can be mixed up and if you are happy to grill it instead of using the oven, everything can be cooked all in one pan. You will still need to spoon it out of the pan to serve but it's one less item to wash up.

Veggie CON BEANIE

1 tbsp olive oil

1 onion, peeled and diced

2 garlic cloves, peeled and chopped

2 carrots, peeled and thinly sliced

1 fresh chilli, deseeded and sliced

400g tin baked beans

400g tin five-bean salad, drained

200g chopped tomatoes

198g tin sweetcorn, drained

1 tbsp soy sauce

1 tsp paprika

2 tbsp tomato purée

pinch of caster sugar

1 tsp mild chilli powder

salt and pepper

150ml water

300g long grain rice

4 tbsp soured cream

handful of chopped fresh parsley

This is another one for the veggies and is a twist on a chilli. It's so great to throw together that you can concentrate on getting the flavour of the chilli exactly to your liking. Colourful, filling, yummy and healthy – chuck it in a pot and go, go, go!

1. Heat the olive oil in a large saucepan over a medium heat, add the onion and fry for 3–4 minutes. Tip in the garlic, carrots and chilli and cook for a further 5 minutes.

2. Chuck in both beans, the tomatoes and sweetcorn, stirring to combine, then add the soy sauce, paprika, tomato purée, sugar, chilli powder and a good seasoning of salt and pepper. Taste and tweak to your liking.

3. Add half the water, then leave to simmer for 30 minutes, while you crack on with cooking the rice.

4. Bring a saucepan of water to the boil, add the rice and cook according to the packet instructions – make sure you've given the rice a gentle wash first to remove excess starch and prevent it sticking.

5. The chilli mixture should be nice and thick by now, so adjust with more water or leave to simmer for a bit longer to reduce. Adjust the seasoning if necessary, then serve piled on top of the cooked rice with a good dollop of soured cream and sprinkling of chopped parsley.

Why not try...

Making a meaty version by browning some mince or sausage slices before adding the beans to the pan?

Barry's Tip

You really can't go wrong with this recipe; spend your time getting the flavours and texture of the chilli the way you want it and feel free to experiment – maybe add some dark chocolate in there.

Broccoli
PESTO
SPAGHETTI

150g broccoli florets

300g fresh spaghetti (find in the chiller section in supermarkets)

50g toasted cashew nuts

20g fresh basil leaves, plus extra to garnish

15g Parmesan, plus Parmesan shavings, to serve (optional)

4 tbsp olive oil

½ garlic clove, peeled

juice of 1 lemon

salt

To serve:

ciabatta, toasted

Barry's Tip
This dish is great hot or cold, so why not make a good large batch and take some to work and impress your colleagues with your awesome lunch — then tell them to buy this book and that you aren't on commission...

Words can't really justify how this tastes for such a simple recipe. Broccoli is one of those vegetables that I try to get the kids eating as much as I can, and it's always great to find cool ways to serve it up — but this recipe works for kids of all ages, and can be made in no time at all. When you eat it you get that warm fuzzy feeling and it's just great in every single way.

1. Bring a saucepan of water to the boil and blanch (flashy name for cooking briefly) the broccoli for 90 seconds, then drain and rinse under cold running water to stop it cooking. Set aside. Add the spaghetti to the broccoli cooking water and cook according to the packet instructions.

2. Whizz the cashews, basil, Parmesan, oil and garlic in a mini blender until finely combined. Leave the mixture in the blender.

3. Once the spaghetti is done, drain, reserving a couple of tablespoons of the cooking water in a mug, then return the pasta to the pan, add the pesto mixture and stir well until the pasta is coated evenly all over. If you like to melt the Parmesan in the pesto, pour in a tablespoon of the reserved pasta cooking water; it will also loosen things up.

4. Serve the pasta in a bowl, with extra Parmesan shavings on top if you are feeling extra cheesy, and garnish with some more basil leaves. Serve with toasted ciabatta for extra deliciousness!

Why not try...
Padding out the spaghetti by mixing in some chargrilled vegetables — one of those jars from the supermarket would work a charm — then just warm them in the pan when you add the pesto.

MY *Sexy* VIRGIN MARY SOUP

4 potatoes, peeled and cut into small cubes

1kg tomatoes, skinned and cut in half

1 sweet onion, peeled and cut into wedges

1 garlic clove, peeled and finely chopped

good handful of fresh thyme leaves

1 tbsp olive oil, plus extra for frying

salt and pepper

300ml vegetable stock

½ tsp celery salt

Tabasco sauce

Worcestershire sauce

To serve:

chopped fresh parsley

Barry's Tip

You can adjust the thickness of the soup with the amount of stock. If you gradually add the stock to the blender you can get the texture you want – just make sure you get the balance of the sauces right too!

The title says it all – think of a Virgin Mary cocktail (the non-alcoholic version of a Bloody one) made into a soup. Well that's what I've done here and served it with some potato croûtons; it's 'bloomin sexy indeedy' with a nice little kick that you can control to your liking. Good times.

1. Preheat the grill to Medium. Bring a pan of water to the boil, add the potato cubes and parboil them until softened. Drain and set aside.

2. Meanwhile, mix the tomatoes, onion, garlic, thyme and olive oil together in a bowl. Arrange the tomatoes neatly on a tray, spreading them out evenly. Season with salt and pepper, then put them under the grill for 20 minutes or until the tomatoes have softened and are starting to slightly char. You can cook them in the oven if you prefer.

3. Heat a tablespoon of olive oil in a frying pan over a medium heat. Add the potato cubes and pan-fry until golden brown all over. Use tongs to flip them over. Once done, transfer them to a plate and season lightly.

4. When the tomatoes are done, pour the stock into a blender, add the tomatoes and whizz until the tomatoes are completely broken down. The mixture as it is now is actually very yummy, but now is the time to personalise it. Add the celery salt and a couple of shakes of Tabasco and Worcestershire sauce, then whizz, taste and add more until you have got the right amount of 'kick'. A good 10–12 drops of Tabasco and Worcestershire sauce work well, but it's your soup, so tweak it, baby.

5. Serve in a bowl with a handful of the potato croûtons dunked in, some chopped parsley and a good seasoning of salt and pepper.

Why not try...

Going for a full-on Bloody Mary soup by stirring in vodka before serving – not on a school night please!

Vegetable
& LENTIL
CROWD-PLEASER

1 tbsp olive oil

1 large onion, peeled and diced

3 garlic cloves, peeled and finely chopped

1 tsp tomato purée

1 heaped tsp ground cumin

½ tsp ground coriander

1 heaped tsp paprika

3 carrots, peeled and cut into 2.5cm chunks

3 parsnips, peeled and cut into 2.5cm chunks

300g sweet potato, peeled and cut into 2.5cm chunks

400g small potatoes of your choice, peeled and cut into 2.5cm chunks

400g tin tomatoes

1 litre vegetable stock

150g red lentils

salt and pepper

good handful of chopped fresh parsley, for sprinkling

To serve:

crusty buttered bread

This dish is just perfect – it's a simple, delicious, wholesome, one-pot filler that will load your boots with healthy nosh! The base is spiced relatively mild for you to ramp up to your liking, but as it is the textures and flavours of the veg work a treat with the lentils. Great for people of all ages!

1. Heat the olive oil in a large frying pan over a medium heat, add the onion and fry for 4–5 minutes until softened. Add the garlic and fry for 1 minute. Next, add the tomato purée, cumin, coriander and paprika and heat for a minute, stirring to combine.

2. Add the rest of the ingredients to the pan (one at a time obviously!), then bring to a simmer for a good 30–35 minutes or until all the vegetables have softened. Season to taste and tweak with extra paprika or spices, if you wish, then serve in bowls with a sprinkling of chopped parsley and some crusty buttered bread to dunk – super stuff!

Why not try...
Replacing the red lentils with some seasoned browned cubes of beef for a meaty upgrade?

Barry's Tip
Make sure all the vegetables are cut to a similar size, as dropping a huge potato in there isn't gonna work!

Puy Lentil Salad
WITH ROAST BEETROOT

4 beetroot, peeled and sliced

2 tbsp olive oil, plus extra for cooking

3 tbsp water

salt and pepper

1 tbsp extra-virgin olive oil

1 tbsp hazelnut oil

1 tbsp orange juice or juice of ½ fresh orange

1 tsp honey

20g chopped hazelnuts

1 red onion, peeled and sliced

400g tin Puy lentils, drained

70g bag rocket leaves

100g goat's cheese, cut into chunks

Those of you who have seen some of my videos will know I used to have a fear of beetroot. I'm not sure what it was, perhaps the Dracula-style hands you get when preparing it, but I really love it now. In this salad, beetroot is roasted and served with red onion, Puy lentils and a little goat's cheese – a few years ago you'd never catch me eating this, but there's definitely something lovely about it.

1. Preheat the oven to 180°C/160°C fan/350°F/Gas mark 4.

2. Plonk the beetroot onto a baking tray, add the olive oil and water, then season with salt and pepper. Cover with foil and bake in the oven for a good 45–50 minutes. Halfway through cooking, spoon some of the oil over the beetroot, if you wish.

3. Meanwhile, combine the extra-virgin olive and hazelnut oils, orange juice, honey and a pinch of salt and pepper in a bowl. Taste and tweak until you are happy with the flavour.

4. Toast the hazelnuts gently in a small frying pan over a low heat, keeping the pan moving, until the nuts are golden brown. Set aside.

5. When the beetroot is ready, heat a drop of olive oil in a pan over a medium heat. Add the onion and cook for about 5–7 minutes until softened. Tip them into the beetroot, add the lentils and stir well to combine and warm through.

6. Serve with a good handful of rocket on a plate, topped with the lentil mixture, some small chunks of goat's cheese, the toasted hazelnuts sprinkled over and the dressing drizzled over the top.

Why not try...
Roasting the onions with the beetroot? Add them halfway through the beetroot's cooking time to give an added sweetness boost.

Peasy
OVEN-BAKED
RISOTTO

2 tbsp unsalted butter

3 shallots, peeled and finely chopped

1 garlic clove, peeled and finely chopped

300g risotto rice

150ml white wine

1 litre hot vegetable stock

10 broad beans

1 courgette, sliced into small squares

80g peas

salt and pepper

grated Parmesan, for sprinkling

chopped fresh mint, for sprinkling

Barry's Tip

You might want to add the Parmesan and seasoning to the risotto after serving. I tend to like a lot of Parmesan stirred through mine, but Mrs Barry prefers it lighter.

Spank my hiney and call me Susan! This is one heck of a lovely dish, as it's warm, filling, loving and easy, exactly what you want any time of the day at any time of the year. It's a delicious vegetarian oven-baked risotto that is actually quite unintimidating compared to other risottos, so I hope you give it a try and put your own spin on it.

1. Preheat the oven to 180°C/160°C fan/350°F/Gas mark 4.

2. Melt the butter in a saucepan over a medium heat until bubbling. Tip in the shallots and cook for 5–6 minutes until softened. Add the garlic and cook for a further minute.

3. Stir in the rice, coating it completely in the butter, then add the wine and keep stirring until it is almost absorbed. Pour in the hot vegetable stock and bring to the boil.

4. Once it hits boiling stage, transfer the risotto to an ovenproof dish with a lid, cover and bake in the oven for 20 minutes.

5. Meanwhile, bring a saucepan of water to the boil, add the broad beans and cook for 2 minutes. Drain and dunk the beans into a bowl of ice-cold water, then drain and pop the beans out of their leathery skins into a clean bowl.

6. Take the risotto out of the oven, uncover and add the courgette, broad beans and peas. Stir, then cover with the lid and return to the oven for about 8–10 minutes.

7. When done, season well with salt and pepper, stir through a generous helping of Parmesan and a sprinkling of mint and serve.

Why not try...
Mixing up the fillings any way you choose? You could try different herb combinations or even add some gammon for a little meaty madness.

Spanish (ish) CRISP TORTILLA

6 large eggs

½ tsp pepper

1 tbsp olive oil

1 red onion, peeled and sliced

handful of spinach

50g Cheddar cheese, grated

50g Red Leicester cheese, grated

50g ready salted crisps

To serve:

rocket and herb salad

Okay, so this recipe is a sort of lazy cross between a Spanish omelette and a crisp frittata. It's a super-quick dish to throw together. The fillings can be tweaked to your liking and will definitely plug a gap. Of course, the crisps are the main talking point, but if you want a quick filler, look no further.

1. Crack the eggs into a bowl, add the pepper and beat together until well combined. Set aside.

2. Preheat the grill to Medium. Heat a 15cm frying pan over a medium-high heat and add the olive oil. Once the pan is hot, throw in the onion and cook for about 5 minutes.

3. Tip in the spinach and let it wilt over the heat. This should take no longer than 1 minute.

4. Mix the cheeses together and add half to the beaten eggs. Break up the crisps in their packet(s) (kind of how they were when you took them to school in your bag) and then plonk them into the egg mixture – coating them well.

5. Tip the eggy-crisp mixture into your frying pan and stir to spread out the mix evenly over the base. You will notice that the egg will start to cook, but keep dragging it from the sides with a spatula to draw the raw egg mixture in. After about 3 minutes the base should be pretty much set – you will know as there won't be any raw egg around the edges.

6. Take off the heat and sprinkle the remaining cheese over the top, trying to get it into any puddles of raw egg.

7. Place the pan under the grill and grill for 5 minutes or until the tortilla has set and the cheese is golden.

8. Slide the tortilla onto a chopping board, slice into wedges and serve with a rocket and herb salad.

Why not try...

Adding some cooked meat to the egg mixture? A spicy kick of pepperoni could do it or a Hawaiian version with ham and pineapple pieces.

Barry's Tip

If you want to notice the texture of the crisps rather than just their flavour, add them to the pan with the egg and stir through gently, then add some more with the cheese topping.

Veggie

Falafel HASH

400g tin chickpeas, drained and rinsed

1 garlic clove, peeled

1 heaped tsp ground cumin

1 heaped tsp mild chilli powder

1 heaped tsp paprika

½ red onion, peeled and cut into rough chunks

good handful of fresh coriander, plus extra to garnish

zest and juice of 1 lemon

1 egg

2 tbsp olive oil, plus extra for drizzling

1 tbsp sweet chilli sauce, either shop-bought or see page 219

black pepper

To serve:

side salad

your favourite dressing

pitta bread

Before I started learning to cook I had never tried a specifically vegetarian dish, but loads of people asked me to make some, and what I've found is that there is something about veggie dishes that take them to another level – it's like different dimensions of flavour and texture. In this recipe a falafel hash is whirled together, pan-fried and topped with a poached egg. Add a trickle of sweet chilli sauce – and I just love it!

1. Whizz the chickpeas, garlic, cumin, chilli powder, paprika, red onion, coriander and the zest and juice of three-quarters of the lemon together in a food processor until it forms a lovely colourful pulp of spicy chickpea goodness.

2. Crack the egg into a little pot or cup. Bring a saucepan of water to the boil, then reduce the heat to a simmer.

3. Heat the olive oil in a frying pan, tip in the falafel mixture and, using a spatula, spread it out to cover the base. Cook, stirring, until it starts to brown, about 10 minutes. Take off the heat and hack it up a little.

4. Meanwhile, stir the simmering water to create a little whirlpool, then tip the egg swiftly and confidently into the pan. Poach for 2 minutes or until the egg white is fully cooked through. The whirlpool should help hold the egg together, although don't spin it too fast!

5. Spoon the hash into a serving dish, drizzle over the sweet chilli sauce and squirt the rest of the lemon juice over the top. When the egg is ready, lift out with a slotted spoon and place on the hash pile (sounds illegal). Top with a teaspoon of olive oil, a grinding of pepper and a little extra chopped coriander. Pierce the egg yolk so it dribbles over the hash and mixes with the sweet chilli and lemon juice – these flavours work amazingly together! Serve with a simple side salad, your favourite dressing and pitta bread.

Why not try...

Easing the veggie option by pan-frying some diced chorizo sausage? The chorizo and the lovely spicy oil oozing out over the hash really adds another dimension.

Spiced Squash & COCONUT SOUP

1 butternut squash (about 900g), peeled, deseeded and cut into small chunks

1 tbsp olive oil, plus extra for frying

1 heaped tsp cumin seeds

1 heaped tsp coriander seeds

1 tsp chilli flakes

salt and pepper

1 onion, peeled and diced

1 garlic clove, peeled and finely chopped

500ml vegetable stock

400ml light coconut milk

chopped fresh coriander, to garnish

To serve:

bread

Barry's Tip

Make sure that the lid on your blender is firmly on before whizzing, as you don't want hot soup sprayed all over your kitchen – unless you are a fan of modern art.

Words can't describe how good this soup tastes – it's like a tropical vegetable bowl with a cheeky little kick that you just wanna keep going back to for more. The squash is cut into chunks, spiced, roasted and whizzed with coconut milk to make this lovely dish your new best friend!

1. Preheat the oven to 190°C/170°C fan/375°F/Gas mark 5.

2. Spread out the squash in a roasting tin and coat in the olive oil. Sprinkle on the cumin and coriander seeds, chilli flakes and a pinch of salt and pepper, then, using your hands, toss the squash until it is coated all over in the spices. Roast in the oven for about 30 minutes or until the squash has softened and there's some colour on the edges. This is yummy as a little side dish on its own.

3. Heat a drop of olive oil in a saucepan over a medium heat, add the onion and garlic and fry for 2 minutes or until soft. Tip in the roasted squash, vegetable stock and coconut milk, then lower the heat to just under a simmer and warm slowly, stirring occasionally to incorporate the flavours.

4. Carefully pour the mixture into a blender and whizz until smooth. Season to taste with salt and pepper and add a sprinkling of chopped coriander. It's pretty filling on its own, but of course dunk away with some bread of your choice!

Why not try...
Putting a Halloween-style twist on the recipe by substituting the squash for the pumpkin flesh that you will carve out of the pumpkin.

Wrapatouille

½ aubergine, cut into small 1cm cubes

3 tbsp vegetable oil

1 small courgette, cut in small 1cm cubes

1 onion, sliced thinly

2 garlic cloves, crushed

1 medium green pepper, deseeded and chopped into strips

200g tin chopped tomatoes, drained

1 tbsp red wine vinegar

handful chopped fresh basil leaves

pinch of cayenne pepper

6 wheat flour tortillas

200g Cheddar cheese, grated, plus extra for topping

50g tinned sweetcorn, drained

To serve:

sour cream, salsa and chopped freshly washed lettuce

Not only is ratatouille the second recipe I ever made and also a great kids' movie (Phoebe told me to write that), it's also super-easy to make, cheap, filling, freezable and you can do so much with it. In this recipe it is served in lovely wheat tortillas, with a little sweetcorn crunch and melted-cheese party going on. Great filler this.

1. Over a medium heat, cook the aubergine in 1 tablespoon of oil for about 2 minutes, flipping halfway through. Tip in the courgette with the aubergine and when both veg begin to soften, tip in the onion, garlic and pepper and top up with another tablespoon of oil. Stir occasionally until everything is softened – about another 5 minutes.

2. Next add the tomatoes, vinegar, basil and cayenne pepper, continue to cook over a medium heat, stirring until all combined. This needs to simmer down a little, so give it a good 10 minutes to get rid of any liquid in the pan; if there's not much in there add a couple of tablespoons of water. It should be moist but not liquidy.

3. When the veg is lovely and soft, season to taste, then tip into a mixing bowl. If the vegetables have a lot of juice, drain in a colander.

4. Warm the tortillas in the microwave for 15 seconds, then sprinkle a little cheese in the middle of each one, divide the ratatouille mixture evenly over the top, scatter over the sweetcorn, then finish with more grated cheese.

5. Roll the tortillas from the bottom up, bring the bottom edge to the top, then pull back, bringing the filling with it, fold in the sides/wings, then roll forward until it sits on the seam as one lovely parcel. You'll get better at this with time.

6. Go back to your pan from earlier, give it a wipe and warm up a tablespoon of oil over a medium heat. Once hot, cook the parcels roughly 2 minutes either side or until golden brown. They will give off a lovely smell as they cook. Depending on the size of your pan you may want to do this step one at a time or in batches.

7. Slice the wraps down the middle diagonally and serve with some chopped lettuce and pots of sour cream and tomato salsa for dipping.

Aubergine & SPINACH MADRAS WARMER

This recipe is a little favourite of mine. I enjoy watching Bristol Rugby Club and it gets pretty cold on those terraces, so there's nothing better to warm me up afterwards than whacking this together in a pot, jumping in the bath while it bubbles away and then eating it while watching TV – delicious!

1 tbsp olive oil

1 red onion, peeled and finely sliced

2 garlic cloves, peeled and finely chopped

2.5cm piece of fresh ginger, peeled and finely chopped

good handful of fresh coriander, including stalks, chopped

2 tbsp Madras curry paste

400g aubergine, cubed

400g sweet potato, peeled and cubed

400g tin chopped tomatoes

400ml vegetable stock

60g fresh spinach

salt and pepper

To serve:

rice

1. Heat the olive oil in a large saucepan, add the onion and fry for 5 minutes to soften. Add the garlic and ginger, stalks of the coriander and the curry paste and fry for a minute, stirring to incorporate.

2. Add the aubergine, sweet potato, tomatoes and stock, then bring to the boil. Lower the heat and simmer for 25 minutes to reduce slightly and soften the vegetables, adding the spinach at the end to wilt.

3. Season well, sprinkle the coriander leaves over the top and serve on its own as a warming veggie filler or alongside some rice for a substantially gorgeous curry.

Why not try...
Blending the mixture up as a curry soup and taking it on your travels?

Barry's Tip
This curry has a bit of kick, but you can adjust the strength by adding less spices at the start and, of course, using a particular curry paste. There's a whole range of pastes available at most supermarkets, in a variety of strengths.

DESSERTS

⚡

RHUBARB & LEMON CREAM SCONES
NUTELLA BAGEL PUDDING
PITY DA FOOL FOOL
PARADISE PUDDING
TERRY'S CHOCOLATE ORANGE BROWNIES
EASY PEACH & APPLE LATTICE PIE
YOLO SALTED CARAMEL MOUSSE
LIME & PASSION FRUIT DRIZZLE CAKE
LEMON POPPYSEED MUFFINS
VANILLA ICE-CUBE TRAY ROCKY ROAD
'FRODO CONES' VANILLA & HONEYCOMB SEMIFREDDO CONES
MOCHA TIRAMISU
CHOCOLATE DUMBBELL TRUFFLES
BANOFFEE COFFEE BREAD
BLACK FOREST ROULADE
ENCASED WHITE CHOCOLATE & RASPBERRY CHEESECAKE

Rhubarb
& Lemon Cream
Scones

50g butter, cold and cut into mini cubes, plus extra for greasing

220g self-raising flour, plus extra for dusting

pinch of salt

1 heaped tsp baking powder

2 tbsp caster sugar

40g currants

150ml semi-skimmed milk, at room temperature

1 tsp vanilla extract

1 egg, beaten

Lemon cream:

300ml whipping cream

2 tbsp caster sugar

2½ tbsp lemon curd

lemon zest and/or juice (optional)

Barry's Tip
Don't knead the dough too much – we aren't making a loaf of bread; it's just to get it nice and smooth.

I've grown up on a relatively good amount of scones, living close to Cheddar (where the cheese originates from). I'd often go there as a child and have freshly baked ones smothered in clotted cream and strawberry jam. Well, there's no way I want to compete with those babies, so I had this idea to merge one of my favourite sweets as a child – rhubarb and custard – with the nostalgic scones, and, oh, these are good.

1. Preheat the oven to 200°C/180°C fan/400°F/Gas mark 6 and lightly grease and flour a baking tray. Put the butter into a mixing bowl and sift in the flour, salt and baking powder. Using your fingertips, work the butter into the dry ingredients to create a crumblike texture – this makes my fingers tingle for some reason!

2. Add the sugar and currants and stir in gently with a spoon, then push the mixture down to form a little well. Pour in the milk and vanilla and, using a fork, work the mix to make a dough. It should be a little sticky so plonk on a floured surface and knead gently until smooth.

3. Roll out the dough carefully on the floured surface to about 1–2cm thick, then, using round cutters (a 5 or 6cm cutter works well), cut into neat rounds.

4. Put the scone rounds onto the prepared baking tray, then use a pastry brush to coat the tops with beaten egg. Bake in the oven for 14–16 minutes. The scones should be golden brown and risen once done. Allow to cool.

cont...

Rhubarb & LEMON CREAM SCONES cont.

Rhubarb:

400g rhubarb, cut into small pieces

100g caster sugar (tweak to taste)

2 tbsp water

juice of ½ lemon

5. Put the rhubarb, sugar, water and lemon juice in a separate saucepan over a low heat. Cover with a lid and cook, stirring occasionally, for 10 minutes until completely broken down. Take out half of the rhubarb mixture and blitz until smooth. Return to the pan and allow to cool until needed.

6. Meanwhile, for the lemon cream, using an electric whisk, whip the cream and sugar together until slightly thickened and combined. Stir through the lemon curd with a spatula (add the curd gradually to your liking), then add some lemon zest/juice if you wish. Chill in the fridge until needed.

7. Serve the scones with a good dollop of the rhubarb spooned onto one scone half, a nice cushion of lemon cream dolloped over the top, then the other scone half-rested on for the lid. You can serve the scones slightly warm, but obviously the cream won't like this, much better cold!

Why not try...

Taking the lemon flavour up a notch with a little added zest or juice into the scone mix or even some lemon peel with the currants? Don't let the rhubarb feel left out, though!

Nutella BAGEL PUDDING

unsalted butter, for greasing

4 bagels, ideally left out overnight (slightly stale, don't leave them outside your house)

small tub of Nutella

100g chopped hazelnuts

30g chocolate chips

3 large eggs, beaten

100ml double cream, at room temperature

250ml semi-skimmed milk, at room temperature

60g caster sugar

pinch of salt

1 tbsp chocolate Nesquik powder

ice cream or Honeycomb Semifreddo (see page 195), to serve

Barry's Tip
Please keep your eye on the pudding when it's in the oven without a foil covering, as you don't want any burnt chocolate or bread going on.

This idea came about when I was in the car with my good friend Mark Caperton singing along to Peter Andre's 'Mysterious Girl'. We took a break from singing and discussed our favourite foods, the popular stuff like curries and burgers were mentioned, but Nutella, bread and butter pudding and bagels kept coming back into the conversation, so after a little brainstorm I came up with this – a chocolate-hazelnut bread and butter pudding using bagels. Very, very naughty.

1. Butter a 2lb loaf tin. Halve the bagels and spread a layer of Nutella on each piece. Cut each slice into quarters and dip into the chopped hazelnuts. You may have an urge to eat these!

2. Wedge the bagel pieces into the prepared loaf tin, building up the layers as you go and sprinkling the chocolate chips in between.

3. Put the eggs, cream, milk, sugar, salt and chocolate milkshake powder into a jug and mix until well combined. Pour over the pudding evenly; try to coat the tops a little and then leave to soak for 20 minutes.

4. Meanwhile, preheat the oven to 180°C/160°C fan/350°F/Gas mark 4. Bake the pudding in the oven for 15 minutes, uncovered, or until the top is firm and the hazelnuts are roasted. At this point, take out of the oven and cover the top with foil, then continue to bake for a good 30–35 minutes or until set. Allow to cool for a few minutes, then serve with ice cream, or if you are feeling extra cheeky, the Honeycomb Semifreddo on page 199.

Why not try...
Putting some marmalade and orange peel in the pudding with the chocolate chips to satisfy any chocolate-orange cravings you may have, or is that just me?

Pity DA FOOL FOOL

100g caster sugar

100g unsalted peanuts

pinch of salt

100g milk chocolate, broken into small blocks

4 meringue nests

300ml double cream

70g milk chocolate, chopped finely

There's nothing better than a super-naughty dessert every now and again – as long as you share, of course. This Snickers-inspired fool is crammed full of chocolate chips, peanut brittle and meringue and surrounded by a lightly whipped cream. It's delicious and you'd be a crazy fool if you don't give it a try!

1. First make the peanut brittle. Put a non-stick pan over a very low heat and tip in the sugar evenly. Don't touch it; it'll take around 10 minutes before anything happens, then you'll notice a caramel pool appearing, with lumps of white sugar sat on top. At this stage, still over a low heat, mix in the sugar with a spatula, combining everything until it all forms a lovely caramel lake. Tip in the peanuts and a pinch of salt and stir through briefly. Once everything is coated, tip into a silicone tray or buttered baking sheet, spread evenly with the spatula and allow to cool fully – it'll only take 15 minutes or so to cool and harden.

2. Melt the 100g of chocolate in a microwave in 20-second blasts, stirring in between. Allow to cool to room temperature.

3. When completely cool, put the peanut brittle in a sealable bag and bash it into chunks. In a separate bag, bash up the meringue nests into small chunks.

4. Whisk the cream in a bowl until soft peaks form and then, using a metal spoon, fold in the brittle, meringue pieces, chocolate chips and a good tablespoon of melted chocolate. Try not to overfold the mixture.

5. Spoon carefully between two glasses and place in the fridge until ready to serve – give it at least 30 minutes to chill.

6. Before serving, drizzle over some leftover melted chocolate, and sprinkle the remaining finely chopped chocolate, meringue or brittle.

Why not try...

If you're scared of making brittle yourself (burning sugar is dangerous!), just buy some from your local shop, or you could even leave the nuts separately bashed and mix in a tin of ready-made caramel. It's also easier to make more brittle; the quantities used here are just for this recipe, but if you double or treble them you'll get a bigger caramel lake, making it easier to coat the nuts.

Barry's Tip

You'll see that here I've made sure everything is prepared – and most importantly cool – before assembling. Chucking in hot or even warm ingredients will not make your cream stiff. So keep it cool and fold only as much as you need to.

Paradise PUDDING

Difficulty ●●
Ready in **1 HOUR 10 MINUTES**
Serves **6**

700ml semi-skimmed milk

400ml tin reduced-fat coconut milk

130g pudding rice or arborio rice

80g caster sugar, plus about 2 tbsp for compote

1 tsp ground nutmeg

1 vanilla pod

½ tbsp butter, cut into small cubes

1 mango, cut into chunks

1 peach, sliced

pulp of 1 passion fruit

juice of 1 orange

My nan used to make the best rice puddings. I'd have one every Sunday after roast dinner without fail and they're just amazingly scrummy – great for baby food too. For this recipe the dish gets a slightly exotic vibe with a delicious compote (vision of my nan drinking out of a coconut), giving a taste combo that's coconut creamy and dreamy!

1. Preheat the oven to 180°C/160°C fan/350°F/Gas mark 4. Put both milks, the rice, sugar and nutmeg in a saucepan over a medium heat and stir to combine. Cut the vanilla pod in half lengthways, scrape out the seeds with the tip of the knife and plonk the seeds and pod into the mixture. Keep stirring for just over 5 minutes until simmering, then turn off the heat and discard the pod.

2. Carefully transfer the mixture to a 1.4-litre shallow baking dish, top with a couple of dabs of butter and bake in the oven for 20 minutes. Take out of the oven, stir well, then return to the oven for a further 30–40 minutes until a skin has formed on top and the rice is lovely and creamy underneath.

3. Meanwhile, make the compote. Put the mango, peach and passion fruit pulp in a saucepan over a medium heat. Squeeze in the orange juice, then stir in the 2 tablespoons of sugar and leave until it is at a low simmer. Simmer gently, stirring occasionally, for about 10 minutes, adding extra sugar if needed and squishing the fruit with the back of a spatula. Once you're happy with the consistency, pour into a jug and allow to cool. (If you don't want the passion-fruit seeds, pour the mixture through a sieve into the jug, although they do look cool.)

4. Serve the rice pudding warm, if you like. I actually prefer mine cold (just the way I used to eat it, I guess!) with a dollop of compote on top.

Why not try...

Adding fruit to the rice mixture before putting it in the oven? Raisins and sultanas work great, or even some griddled pineapple.

Barry's Tip
If you would rather not fork out on a vanilla pod (they are expensive, but worth it), use a drop of vanilla extract instead.

Terry's Chocolate Orange **BROWNIES**

280g dark chocolate, roughly broken

280g unsalted butter at room temperature

1½ tsp orange essence

zest of 1 orange

5 large eggs

420g caster sugar

60g cocoa powder

120g plain flour

8–9 Terry's Chocolate Orange segments

To serve:

crème fraîche or ice cream

I love Terry's Chocolate Orange (and I'm not being paid to write that!). Every Christmas Day I've had one for breakfast since the age of 5 – and that's a tradition I'm definitely passing on to my girls. This recipe combines this affection with some good old chocolate brownies, which to be fair aren't too shabby either – add in a drop of orange essence and you've got a whole lot of orange-chocolate-loving right there.

1. Preheat the oven to 180°C/160°C fan/350°F/Gas mark 4.

2. Put the broken chocolate and butter in a microwaveable bowl and melt in the microwave in 20-second blasts, stirring in between until fully combined and looking like the chocolate lake from *Charlie and the Chocolate Factory* – about 80 seconds in total. Mix in the orange essence and zest, then allow to cool slightly. If you don't have a microwave, you can do this using a heatproof bowl over a pan of simmering water.

3. Cream together the eggs and sugar in a separate bowl, using either a balloon whisk (much respect) or an electric whisk – do this for at least 5 minutes until it's changed to a pale colour and has thickened.

4. Now fold the chocolate mixture into the creamed sugary eggs. I know you'll see me raving about spatulas through this book, but they are great for scraping everything off the bowl and that's what you need to do here. Scrape it down and fold through to get some air in there until really well combined.

5. Your bowl will now look like a dark chocolate protest, sift the dry bits into it – the cocoa powder and flour – then fold through again. It'll be a bit thicker, looking like a chocolate cement, but keep folding until fully combined.

7. In a prepared (greased and lined) 20cm square tray or brownie tin, if you have one, pour in half of the batter mixture, then position the chocolate orange segments in the middle of the square areas you intend to cut once they are done – leave an even gap between the edges of the tray and the chocolate orange pieces. Once happy with the tactical layout of your orange pieces, pour the remaining batter on top and bake on the middle shelf for a good 35 minutes.

cont...

8. Don't be tempted to take the brownies out too soon; the top will firm up quite early on but you want to focus just as much on the sides, if you see they are coming away from the tray/greaseproof lining, it's a good sign they are nearly done.

9. Once you are confident they are done, remove from the oven and, this is the hard bit, just leave them! Let them cool down fully, as they'll still be cooking away inside. Cut the brownies up into squares straight from the tin, or if you prefer, lift them out using the greaseproof paper and cut them up on a chopping board. Serve with some crème fraîche or ice cream.

Why not try...

Switching up the dark chocolate with milk chocolate or white chocolate chips to add a cool colour dimension to the brownie batter? You could also try an After Eight version by replacing the Chocolate Orange pieces with After Eight ones and the orange essence with peppermint essence.

Barry's Tip

Ensure the chocolate orange bits are covered right up by the brownie batter – we don't want them getting too exposed in there. Also, when microwaving the chocolate don't overdo it – scorched chocolate stinks! There is residual (what a cool word) heat when you take it out of the microwave, so when you stir it it's still melting – be careful.

Easy
PEACH & APPLE LATTICE PIE

500g block chilled ready-made shortcrust pastry

20g plain flour, plus extra for dusting

400g peach slices from a tin, drained (or use fresh if you prefer)

2 large cooking apples, peeled and thinly sliced (about 600g)

50g caster sugar, plus extra for sprinkling

milk, for brushing

To serve:

good-quality vanilla ice cream

Barry's Tip
If you don't fancy making a lattice, just roll out a second disc of pastry and put it on top as a classic pie.

There's nothing quite like a nice fruit-filled pie, so I've crammed two of my favourite fruits into this one. I have also made it ridiculously simple by using awesome shop-bought pastry; don't get me wrong, making pastry from scratch is fun and messy, but for an impressive quick hit this emergency pudding works a treat.

1. Preheat the oven to 190°C/170°C fan/375°F/Gas mark 5.

2. Divide the pastry into 2 portions. You will need roughly two-thirds for the base and edges and the rest for the lattice topping. Using a floured rolling pin, roll out the larger portion of pastry on a lightly floured board – make sure it's wide enough to allow for the edges and a little shrinkage – then lift it into a 22cm, 4–5cm deep pie dish, carefully pushing into the corners all the way round. Overlapping is fine as it will be trimmed later. Put in the fridge. Roll out your remaining pastry and, using a pasta cutter (it gives a cool pattern effect, but a knife is fine), cut out long strips to go along your pie. You will need about 10 of equal width. Sit these on a baking sheet or chopping board and chill in the fridge.

3. Lay the peach and apple slices evenly between sheets of kitchen paper and pat dry gently. Put the sugar and flour in a large bowl, add all the fruit and mix together lightly with a spatula. Try not to hack the fruit up too much.

4. Remove the pastry from the fridge and pile the fruit high into the dish. It looks a lot but will reduce down as it cooks.

5. Using your pastry strips, form lines over the pie, then rotate your dish 90 degrees and carefully weave in the remaining strips until the top is covered. Press the pastry together to seal, then trim the edge with a sharp knife. Brush all over with milk, sprinkle with sugar and bake in the oven for 30–35 minutes until golden brown. Serve with some good-quality vanilla ice cream.

Why not try...
Slicing the peaches in half and sitting them on their bottoms, then forming the lattice around them to create a cool peach grid?

YOLO SALTED CARAMEL *Mousse*

For the mousse:

130g plain chocolate, broken into squares

4 eggs, separated

1 tbsp caster sugar

For the salted caramel:

240g caster sugar

80ml water

110g unsalted butter

pinch of salt, or more to taste

150ml double cream

For the topping:

250ml double cream

few Rolos, refrigerated

Barry's Tip

Make sure the chocolate mixture is cold before adding the yolks – you really don't want scrambled-egg pudding.

This is a delightfully yummy dessert that gives your taste-buds a real wake-up call. YOLO (you only live once) is definitely a motto to go with this pudding, and it rhymes with a key ingredient it's being modelled on – Rolo! Salted caramel gives it a further edge and it's a great make-ahead dessert for impressing chums.

1. Make the mousse by microwaving the chocolate in a heatproof bowl in 20-second blasts until melted. Allow to cool for a few minutes, then stir through the egg yolks until combined. In a separate bowl, whisk the egg whites until just peaking, then work in the sugar until fully mixed and stiff peaks remain.

2. Gradually fold the egg white into the chocolate mixture, then pour into your serving glasses or jars and refrigerate until slightly set. This mousse is actually very rich, so you may want to serve it in smaller espresso-style cups.

3. For the salted caramel, put the sugar and water in a saucepan and whisk gently over a medium heat until the sugar has dissolved. Lower the heat and let it bubble gently, without stirring, until it is a lovely caramel colour.

4. Take the pan off the heat and add the butter, salt and cream and continue to whisk carefully; it will bubble a little, so watch out. Once everything is mixed in, return the pan to a low heat and simmer gently for 2–3 minutes, making sure you're happy with the texture. Pour the caramel into a bowl and leave to cool, adding more salt, if you like.

5. Meanwhile, for the topping, whip the cream with an electric whisk until soft peaks form and set aside.

6. Cut the chilled Rolos into rough quarters or chunks.

7. When you are ready to build the dessert, take the mousse out of the fridge and carefully pour the salted caramel on top. Top with the whipped cream either as another layer or as a little island, then put the Rolos on top and chill for at least 45 minutes before tucking in.

Why not try...

Adding an extra layer of texture? If you have any leftover cake, cut some into cubes and wedge them first in the bottom of the glass.

Lime
& PASSION FRUIT
DRIZZLE CAKE

175g unsalted butter

175g caster sugar, plus 90g for the icing

3 eggs

2 limes, zest of both and juice of 1

3 passion fruit

200g self-raising flour

icing sugar, for dusting (optional)

Phoebe and I love making cakes together; she's better at making them than I am and could crack eggs when she was two! One of our favourite things to make is a drizzle cake – there's something about the sponge being soaked in a little zingy vibe that works. This is one of our favourite combos: lime and passion fruit – they go really well together. Hope you like this as much as we do!

1. Preheat the oven to 180°C/160°C fan/350°F/Gas mark 4 and line a 2-litre loaf tin with baking parchment.

2. Using an electric whisk, cream the butter and 200g of the sugar together, then tip in the eggs, zest of 1 lime and pulp from 2 of the passion fruits (strain through a sieve and reserve the seeds) and mix until combined. Fold in the flour.

3. Tip the mixture into the prepared loaf tin and bake in the oven for a good 40 minutes until golden brown on top. Insert a skewer in a few places and see if it comes out clean to make sure it's cooked through.

4. While the cake is cooling in the tin, mix together the remaining sugar, zest from the other lime, juice from 1 of the limes, juice from the remaining passion fruit (pass it through a sieve again) and any leftover passion fruit seeds until a polka-dot-type smooth paste is formed. Pierce holes all over the cake with a bamboo skewer, then pour the drizzle over the cake.

5. Once the cake has cooled, dust with icing sugar, if you wish, slice and eat!

Why not try...
Mixing up the zesty-ness? You can use oranges as well as the traditional lemon for different-style drizzle cakes that still have that zing.

Barry's Tip
Make sure that the cake is fully cooked through by testing with a skewer in several different spots. It sounds pretty basic but it can be a pretty horrible feeling cutting into an uncooked cake!

Lemon POPPYSEED MUFFINS

125ml milk

30g melted butter

1 large egg

40ml lemon juice

100g caster sugar

2 tsp lemon zest

175g self-raising flour

1 tbsp poppyseeds

small jar of lemon curd

For the meringue:

2 large egg whites, at room temperature

100g caster sugar

Not only do these cakes look impressive, but they are officially – and you can quote me on this – 'stonking'. A crispy meringue layer to break through initially, then a great lemon poppyseed cake hits you before following up with an even more lemony curd hit. These work really well, and for the majority Phoebe made them with me, and although it does get a little tricky towards the end, it's definitely worth it.

1. Preheat the oven to 200°C/180°C fan/400°F/Gas mark 6 and put 6 muffin cases into a muffin tray.

2. In a mixing bowl pour in the milk and butter, then crack in the egg – both the white and yolk – and add the lemon juice. Mix well together with a spoon until combined.

3. In another bowl, combine the remaining muffin ingredients. Pour in the sugar and lemon zest first of all and stir together with a spoon to merge slightly – you can use your hands if you like to create a wicked lemony sugar. Next, grab a sieve and sift in the self-raising flour, then follow up by tipping in the poppyseeds, stirring together well.

4. It's time to merge the dry and the wet, so pour the wet egg mixture into the dry bowl and give it a good stir until fully combined. Spoon the cake batter halfway up the cases and bake in the oven for 20 minutes or until firm and a toothpick inserted comes out clean (I've always wanted to write that!).

Difficulty ●●●
Ready in **30 MINUTES + COOLING TIME**
Serves **6**

5. Allow the muffins to cool on a rack, meanwhile whisk the room-temperature egg whites until soft peaks form, ideally using an electric whisk, or use a balloon one if you want to work on your guns. Add the sugar gradually until stiff peaks are formed and the mixture looks slightly glossy.

6. Take the muffins out of their cases and make an incision with the knife through the muffin along the base of the lid. Spread with a good amount of lemon curd, then replace the lid back on top like a sort of cake hat.

7. Next, grab the meringue mix and spoon on top of the muffin lids – if you have a piping bag you could make some great shapes. Spoon it all over initially with the teaspoon, then lift lightly in small areas with the back of the spoon to form mini peaks – if the meringues are stiff enough it's pretty easy to do and will look great.

8. Finally, if you haven't got a chef's torch (randomly, I do) to brown the lids, as an alternative place them under the grill briefly to give a lovely golden effect. Keep your eye on them under the grill as it won't take very long at all. That's it, they look pretty impressive and it's now time to eat them!

Barry's Tip

If you're not confident cutting the muffins straight, keep them in their cases first and use the top of the case as a guideline to cut along. Make an initial incision deep into the lid and, rather than moving the knife, move the muffin with your finger and thumb as you spin it – this'll make the lid come clean off.

Why not try...

An orange alternative? Swap the lemon zest and juice with that of an orange, and get hold of some marmalade instead of lemon curd – you could even add orange essence to make it a real orange fest.

100g butter, cut into cubes

200g dark chocolate, broken into pieces

2 tbsp caster sugar

2 tbsp cocoa powder

1 tsp anilla extract

1 tbsp golden syrup

200g digestive biscuits

100g Maltesers

100g marshmallows, chopped

1 tbsp dessicated coconut

50g white chocolate chips, chopped

50g milk chocolate chips, chopped

icing sugar, for dusting

Barry's Tip

This works best when using a silicone or more flexible ice-cube tray. If you have got any mixture left over, put some in greased ramekins to make little rocky road pies.

This is both an amazing rocky road recipe and a very cool concept. Ice-cube trays can be used for lots of great things (including storing herbs in butter in the freezer), but by making our rocky road in there it creates little bite-size portions that are both simple to store and share, avoiding the 'you've got more than me' argument!

1. Put the butter, dark chocolate, caster sugar, cocoa powder, vanilla extract and golden syrup in a saucepan over a medium heat and stir until melted and well combined. Allow to cool to room temperature.

2. Meanwhile, bash up the biscuits in a sealable bag until they form chunky crumbs.

3. In a large mixing bowl, plonk the Maltesers, marshmallows, coconut, chocolate chips and biscuits and stir briefly.

4. Pour the chocolate mixture over the ingredients in the bowl and, using a spatula, work it all around the bowl, scraping the edges and lifting any crumbs from the bottom, stirring until everything is coated in the chocolate.

5. Spoon the mixture into the ice-cube tray, filling each space completely – if there is enough of a lip on your tray, spoon a light layer over all the sections to create a base.

6. Place in the fridge to chill and set for a good 2 hours, or leave overnight. Once ready to serve, push out the pieces of the ice-cube tray and dust with icing sugar, then eat.

Why not try...
Adding a little orange extract instead to the mixture for a chocolate –orange kick? Very nice.

Vanilla ICE-CUBE TRAY ROCKY ROAD

'Frodo Cones'
VANILLA & HONEYCOMB SEMIFREDDO CONES

4 egg yolks

1 vanilla pod, split in half lengthways and seeds scraped out

130g caster sugar

300ml double cream

130g crème fraîche

4 good chunks of honeycomb, bashed into small pieces, plus extra to serve

To serve:

ice-cream cones

handful of bashed hazelnuts

Barry's Tip
If you want to serve it in slices, line the tin with some cling film to make it easier to remove, then slice away, scattering honeycomb over the slices.

Well this has nothing to do with *The Lord of the Rings*, other than 'Frodo' which used to be one of my many nicknames at work due to my hairstyle! Semifreddo is an Italian-style ice cream that's more like a frozen mousse. It's very easy to make, plus you can switch it up in so many ways. Typically served in slices, here it is served like a good-old-fashioned ice cream – in cones dunked in extra honeycomb and bashed hazelnuts.

1. Place the egg yolks, vanilla seeds and caster sugar in a heatproof bowl set over a pan of simmering water over a low heat. Make sure the water doesn't touch the bottom of the bowl. Whisk until slightly thickened and the colour becomes slightly paler – it should be at least double in volume, so 6–7 minutes should do it. Allow to cool.

2. In a separate bowl, whip the cream until slightly thickened then gradually add the crème fraîche and honeycomb pieces until well combined.

3. Go back to the cooled egg-yolk mixture and, using an electric whisk, mix until noticeably thicker, about 4 minutes. Put the cream mixture into the whisked yolks and, using a spatula, fold in gently until well combined.

4. Tip the mixture into the tin (at least 1 litre in size, but it doesn't matter if larger) and freeze for a good 5 hours, or ideally overnight, until set.

5. When ready to serve, scoop into ice-cream cones and roll in the extra bashed honeycomb and hazelnuts, which will stick to the tops, then munch away. Gorgeous!

Why not try...
Putting your creativity to the test by trying out your favourite fillings? Maybe a chocolate, fruit and nut one using raisins and choc chips would tickle your fancy? Good times!

Mocha TIRAMISU

570ml double cream

250g mascarpone (how do you hide an animal? – mascarpone)

45g caster sugar

30g light brown sugar

200g trifle sponge fingers

5 tsp espresso powder mixed with 350ml hot water

60g plain chocolate (at least 70% cocoa solids), finely grated

cocoa powder, for dusting

I have always known what tiramisu is, but I always thought it was some mystical dish to conquer – I'm glad to say that this isn't the case. This is an extremely naughty, mocha-fuelled pudding that you'll want to tap-dance all over, and best of all it's super-easy. Make it and love it!

1. In a mixing bowl whip the double cream, mascarpone and both sugars together with an electric whisk until thick.

2. Swiftly dunk the sponge fingers into the coffee mixture, then arrange in the base of your dish until covered (or you can use individual serving glasses).

3. Spoon half the cream mixture on top and spread to evenly cover, then sprinkle over half the grated chocolate.

4. Put another layer of fingers on top of the cream and grated chocolate layers, then cover with more cream. Chill in the fridge for at least 3–4 hours, but preferably overnight.

5. When you are ready to serve, dust over a little cocoa powder and top with the remaining grated chocolate. Eat a slice, then give some to everyone you know before you eat another piece, then another, then another!

Why not try...

You can't take this dessert too far, but for a change you could triple-layer it, add some orange essence and zest in layers, some nuts, or just put your own twist on it. If you do, send me a picture!

Barry's Tip

Don't dip the sponge fingers into the coffee for too long or they will not come out as one! Increase/decrease the amount of coffee used depending on how strong you like it.

Chocolate
**DUMBBELL
TRUFFLES**

Here I've taken two of my favourite things – Ferrero Rocher and After Eights – and tried to make them into truffle-style balls served on mini skewers to look like weights. I got the idea from cake pops, but whenever I have one of those I always want to eat another, so why not put two on a stick?

Ferrero Rocher

80g low-fat cream cheese

120g Nutella

2 drops vanilla essence

100g wafers

200g chopped hazelnuts

300g milk chocolate

1. Put the cream cheese, Nutella and vanilla essence in a bowl and mix until smooth and combined (don't pick at it!). Put the wafers in a sealable bag and bash with a rolling pin until fine. Add these crumbs to the Nutella mixture, and stir in – it should hold its shape. Get your hands in there and roll the mixture into 16 equal-sized little balls, sit them on a baking tray lined with baking parchment, then place in the fridge to set for 30 minutes at the very least.

2. In the final 5 minutes of chilling, place the chopped hazelnuts on a plate and melt the chocolate, in a bowl set over a pan of simmering water (or in the microwave, if you prefer). Dunk the balls in the chocolate then roll in the hazelnuts. Return to the tray and put back in the fridge to set for another 30 minutes at least.

3. Once the chocolates are all set, thread one truffle onto each end of a cocktail stick to make 8 dumbbells.

cont...

Barry's Tip
Dip the truffles into the chocolate using a bamboo skewer, if you like, as it's a little safer.

Chocolate DUMBBELL TRUFFLES cont.

After Eight

100g low-fat cream cheese

1½ tsp peppermint essence

200g chocolate digestives

150g dark chocolate

icing sugar

1. Mix the cream cheese and ½ teaspoon of the peppermint essence in a bowl until combined; you want to just take the tang off the cheese with a little mint hint so add a little but not too much – they're not Extra Strong mint truffles! Bash the digestives until fine in a sealable bag, using a rolling pin, then add to the cream cheese mixture. As you stir it should hold its shape.

2. Get your hands in there and roll into 16 equal-sized little balls, sit them on a baking tray lined with baking parchment, then place in the fridge to set for 30 minutes at the very least.

3. Melt the dark chocolate with the remaining 1 teaspoon peppermint essence in a bowl set over a pan of simmering water (or in the microwave, if you prefer). Dunk the balls in the chocolate to coat, then return to the tray and put back in the fridge to set.

4. While the truffles set, make up a very simple icing paste by mixing icing sugar with water until a thick paste is formed. Remove the truffles from the fridge, drizzle over a little icing in zigzags, then return to the fridge to completely set.

5. Once the chocolates are all set, thread one truffle onto each end of a cocktail stick to make 8 dumbbells.

Why not try...
If you have an obsession with chocolate orange like I do, make some orange-choc-themed ones with a bit of real orange zest for zing!

Banoffee
COFFEE
BREAD

80g unsalted butter, plus extra for greasing

3 ripe bananas (300g), peeled

170g caster sugar

2 large eggs, beaten

1 tsp baking powder

190g self-raising flour

50g walnuts, roughly chopped, plus a few extra bashed for sprinkling

30g milk chocolate chips

110g bag toffees, such as Werthers Original, chopped into small cubes

100g icing sugar

25ml freshly made black coffee (as strong as you like)

Take banana bread, turn it into banoffee bread, then merge with a coffee-cake glaze and you have an incredibly delicious combination, my friends. As I write this I have a piece next to me so I am tempted to stop typing any...

1. Preheat the oven to 180°C/160°C fan/350°F/Gas mark 4 and butter and line a 1lb loaf tin with greaseproof paper.

2. Mash your nanas (bananas, not old ladies) in a bowl with a fork until squidgy. Meanwhile, in a separate bowl, cream the butter and caster sugar together, until pale and fluffy. Add the eggs and mix to combine. Sift in the baking powder and flour and fold in gently with a spatula. Finally, tip in the good stuff – the mashed bananas, chopped walnuts, chocolate chips and toffee chunks – and mix well until everything is coated in the cake mixture.

3. Pour the mixture into the prepared loaf tin and bake in the oven for 1 hour. After 35–40 minutes it tends to have coloured nicely but won't be cooked through fully, so take it out of the oven, cover the top with foil and continue to bake until a skewer inserted into the middle of the cake comes out clean. Leave the cake to cool.

4. Meanwhile, make a coffee glaze by mixing the icing sugar and coffee together in a bowl. Add more coffee granules if you want a stronger kick, then spread the glaze over the cake. Scatter a strip of bashed walnuts along the glaze, then allow to set before slicing and serving.

Why not try...

Turning these into cupcakes? After cooking, slice in half like the Poppyseed Muffins (see page 194), then add a fresh banana layer with whipped cream.

Barry's Tip

Keep your eye on the cake while it's baking, as you don't want to go to all that effort and then burn the top!

Black FOREST ROULADE

45g cocoa powder, plus extra for sprinkling and dusting

100g caster sugar, plus extra for sprinkling

5 large eggs

¼ tsp baking powder

70g self-raising flour

480ml double cream

4 tbsp cherry cordial

100g cherry jam

200g dark chocolate, chopped into small pieces

9 or so fresh or frozen dark cherries

icing sugar and leftover dark chocolate, grated, to finish (optional)

I absolutely love roulades, in fact that goes for most things that are sweet and rolled up – like Swiss rolls! What I like about the roulade is the lighter feel and the crispy, meringue taste combined with the yummy filling. In this dessert I merge two of my favourite things – roulade and cherries – to make a delicious black forest roulade that goes down a storm.

1. Preheat the oven to 190°C/170°C fan/375°F/Gas mark 5. Line a 35 x 25cm Swiss roll tin with greaseproof paper, then lightly sift some cocoa powder over, enough to thinly cover the paper. Cut out another piece of greaseproof paper that's slightly larger, then sprinkle it with a mixture of caster sugar and cocoa powder and set aside for later.

2. Crack the eggs into a large bowl, add the caster sugar and whisk with an electric whisk until it's light and foamy and full of volume; it may take up to 10 minutes so be patient.

3. Sift the cocoa powder, baking powder and flour over the whisked eggs and gently fold in with a spatula. It should change to a chocolaty colour – don't try not to overfold it, as you need that air in there.

4. Tip the batter into the prepared tin, spreading it evenly, including the corners, then bake on the middle shelf of the oven for about 12–15 minutes or until the top springs back to the touch.

5. Cool for a few minutes, then flip it onto the other cocoa/sugar greaseproof paper. Carefully remove the lining paper and roll the roulade up widthways with the paper inside it for the moment; this will help hold the shape later. Leave to cool.

6. Meanwhile, whip 300ml of the cream to soft peaks, then stir in 2 tablespoons of the cherry cordial until combined. Unroll the roulade and spread the jam over it, leaving about a 1cm border all the way around. Spoon the cherry cream over the top of the jam area – try not to overload the sponge too much as it will spill out of the sides!

cont...

7. Roll up the roulade carefully, using the paper underneath to help you at first. If it cracks it's not a huge deal, as unlike a Swiss roll it will be covered. Leave to rest, ideally seam-side down, in the fridge.

8. Heat the remaining cream gently in a saucepan until it is simmering. Tip in the chopped chocolate, keeping a little back for the decoration, if liked, and turn off the heat. Mix until smooth and shiny and the chocolate has melted. Pour in the remaining cordial and stir again until combined. Allow to cool to room temperature.

9. Take the roulade out of the fridge and spoon over the cherry ganache, spreading it over the sides in a swirling motion to cover. Arrange some dark cherries over the top and dust with a mix of cocoa powder and icing sugar and some grated chocolate, if you like. Now go for a run to make up for the naughtiness you are about to consume.

Why not try...
Switching the cherry cordial in this recipe for an alcoholic kick by adding Kirsch cherry liqueur? Naughty! You could just use the ganache filling all the way through this recipe; I like to look at the different colour contrasts.

Barry's Tip
Don't hesitate when rolling up the roulade; if you see a crack appear that's fine – keep confident, if you stop halfway through rolling it or unravelling it, it won't help!

Encased
WHITE CHOCOLATE & RASPBERRY CHEESECAKE

75g unsalted butter, plus extra for greasing

250g ginger biscuits

50g icing sugar

600g full-fat cream cheese

200ml double cream

200g white chocolate, broken into pieces

6 tbsp raspberry jam

200g fresh raspberries

This is a bit of a crazy concept I came up with when I realised that a homemade biscuit base can go up the side when making a normal cheesecake. So how about taking it one step further by completely encasing a delicious white chocolate raspberry cheesecake in its very own biscuit shell? That's what I've done here, my friends, and trust me, it'll be worth the effort.

1. Grease a 20cm loose-based tin (it needs a depth of about 4.5cm) with a little butter, then melt the remaining butter in a small saucepan. Meanwhile, roughly break up the biscuits in a food processor and blitz until fine crumbs form. Gradually pour in the melted butter until it is fully incorporated into the biscuit crumbs.

2. Press the crumbs into the base and up the sides of the prepared tin, reserving about 100g for the lid. Leave the tin in the fridge to firm up while you prepare the filling.

3. Beat the icing sugar, cream cheese and cream together in a bowl. Melt the white chocolate carefully in a heatproof bowl set over a pan of simmering water, then beat into the cream cheese mix.

4. Remove the tin from the fridge, spread 3 tablespoons of the jam over the biscuit base and scatter over two-thirds of the raspberries, squishing a few with the back of a fork. Spoon the cheesecake mix over the raspberries, then return the tin to the fridge.

5. Warm the remaining raspberry jam, in a pan over a low heat with a teaspoon of water. Stir to loosen the jam then leave to cool slightly. Once the jam mixture has cooled, remove the cheesecake from the fridge and drizzle it over and then, using a knife, fold it through the cheesecake mix in swirls. Push in the remaining raspberries.

6. Let the cheesecake set in the fridge for 1 hour. When just set, remove from the fridge and gently and carefully scatter the remaining crumb mixture on top, joining it up with the sides you have already created.

7. Refrigerate for another 3–4 hours, or overnight would be fine, before cutting into wedges and surprising your guests!

Why not try...
Skipping adding a lid and just make an amazing standard cheesecake?

Barry's Tip
If you are having trouble sealing the edges, try heating up a spoon and using the warm metal to join the bits together.

BITS & BOBS

BARRY'S BURGER BAR
STUFFED BEEF BURGER WITH TOMATO RELISH
PORK & APPLE BURGER WITH CARAMELISED LEEK & ONIONS
MINTED LAMB BURGER WITH MINTY YOGHURT
MIXED BEAN BURGER WITH PORTOBELLO MUSHROOM BUN & SWEETCORN RELISH
CHICKEN AND CHORIZO CIABATTAS WITH SWEET CHILLI RELISH

PICK 'N' MIX SIDES
AVOCADO SALSA
RAINBOW COLESLAW
SWEET POTATO WEDGES
HONEY GLAZED CARROTS
GARLIC BREAD
ORANGE CUMIN RICE

EASY SWEET PASTRY KIT
CINNAMON RAISIN WHIRLS
MAPLE PECAN PLAIT
APPLE & SULTANA WINDMILL
PEACH & STRAWBERRY SQUARES

Barry's
BURGER BAR

Stuffed Beef **BURGER WITH TOMATO RELISH**

Pork & Apple **BURGER WITH CARAMELISED LEEK & ONIONS**

Minted Lamb **BURGER WITH MINTY YOGHURT**

Mixed Bean Burger
WITH PORTOBELLO MUSHROOM BUN & SWEETCORN RELISH

Chicken & Chorizo
CIABATTAS WITH SWEET CHILLI RELISH

Barry's
BURGER BAR

I love a good burger and there's really nothing like homemade ones; knowing exactly what goes in it and making it your way is such a satisfying thing. Here are five different variations to get you going, so feel free to mix and match the breads, relish and fillings to your liking. Serve with chips, a salad or just on their own.

Stuffed Beef
BURGER WITH
TOMATO RELISH

Mix 500g beef mince in a bowl with ½ chopped onion and a small handful of chopped fresh parsley, then season with salt and pepper. Shape into 8 thin, 1cm burger patty shapes, and then sandwich together to make 4 burgers. Plonk a good chunk of torn mozzarella in the centre of half the patties, then sit another patty on top, pressing fingers round the edges to seal – roll it a little, if you like, to make the shape you're after. Put in the fridge for at least 20 minutes to firm up.

Make a simple tomato relish in a pan by combining 5 chopped tomatoes, 1 crushed garlic clove, 2 tablespoons of olive oil, 1 tablespoon of tomato purée and pinches of sugar, salt and pepper to taste. Bring to a boil over a medium heat, then simmer for 12–15 minutes. Cool. Fry the burgers over a medium heat with a drop of olive oil for a good 5 minutes on either side to create a lovely colour.

Serve in toasted buns with the relish, a couple of chunky tomato slices and lettuce.

Pork&Apple
BURGER WITH CARAMELISED
LEEK & ONIONS

Mix 500g pork mince in a bowl with ¼ chopped onion, 2 grated apples, 1 teaspoon of apple sauce, a handful of chopped parsley, a pinch of sage, then season with salt and pepper. Shape the meat into patties and place in the fridge for at least 20 minutes to firm up. Caramelise 1 sliced leek and 1 sliced onion by melting a knob of butter in a pan with 1 teaspoon olive oil, a pinch of sugar and a good tablespoon of cider vinegar. Cook over a medium-low heat for 20 minutes until softened. Set aside. Fry the burgers over a medium heat with a drop of olive oil for 5 minutes each side. Serve in toasted buns with some watercress, a griddled pineapple ring, the pork burger and caramelised mixture on top.

Minted Lamb
BURGER WITH MINTY YOGHURT

Mix 500g lamb mince in a bowl with ½ chopped onion, ½ chopped garlic clove, a pinch of cumin, a good handful of chopped fresh mint and season. Shape the meat into patties and place in the fridge for at least 20 minutes to firm up.

Make the mint relish by mixing a small tub of natural yoghurt with chopped fresh mint and a good season of salt and pepper. Fry the burgers over a medium heat with a drop of olive oil for 5 minutes on each side. Serve in toasted buns with the minty yoghurt, deseeded cucumber chunks/ slithers and some slices of red onion.

Mixed Bean Burger
WITH PORTOBELLO MUSHROOM BUN & SWEETCORN RELISH

Mix a tin of mashed, drained and rinsed kidney beans and and a tin of five beans together with an egg, 80g breadcrumbs, a handful of chopped fresh coriander, 1 teaspoon of chilli powder, 1 teaspoon of paprika, the juice and zest of 1 lime and season with salt and pepper. Shape the mixture into patties and place in the fridge for at least 20 minutes to firm up.

Make the relish – fry ¼ red onion in a pan with a little olive oil to soften, add 150g drained sweetcorn (or fresh), 2 teaspoons of sugar, 50ml rice vinegar and 1 teaspoon of Dijon mustard. Bring to a boil, as for the sweet chilli relish (right), then simmer until thickened and the sweetcorn is coated. Allow to cool.

When ready, fry the burgers over a medium heat with a drop of olive oil for 5 minutes on each side.

Snip off the stalk of a portobello mushroom, drizzle in a little oil and season. Roast on a tray for 10 minutes. Top the mushroom with some sweetcorn relish, some baby gem lettuce and the bean burger, give a light sprinkle of grated Cheddar cheese, then give a quick grill to melt over. Top with some chopped fresh coriander.

Chicken & Chorizo
CIABATTAS WITH SWEET CHILLI RELISH

Make the relish by blending together 180g red chillies (deseed at least half of them), with 1 garlic clove. Pour this into a saucepan with 250ml rice vinegar and 220g caster sugar over a medium heat, stirring until dissolved and combined. Bring to the boil, then turn down and simmer for 25 minutes or until thickened. Allow to cool.

Mix 4 chicken breast fillets with 2 tablespoons of olive oil, a good squirt of lemon juice and some zest. Place on a griddle over a medium heat for 5 minutes on each side. Take out and griddle 8–10 chorizo slices for 1–2 minutes to soften up and release their oils.

To serve, toast ciabatta halves until lightly brown in the toaster, cover each half with a slice of cheese, whack under the grill to melt for a few minutes before topping with rocket leaves, relish, chicken pieces, chorizo, another squirt of lemon and a sprinkling of parsley.

Barry tip...
Cooking times for meat are a guideline only; please always check they are fully cooked before serving – no pink bits in the middle!

Pick 'n' Mix
SIDES

Avocado SALSA

1 red onion, finely chopped

2 tomatoes, roughly chopped

1 ripe avocado, peeled, stoned and diced

Juice of ½ a lemon

handful fresh coriander, roughly chopped

½ tsp mild chilli powder

salt and pepper

1. Combine all the ingredients in a bowl and mix well. Use your fork to mash the avocado a bit.

2. Season and tweak the flavourings to taste.

3. Refrigerate until needed.

Rainbow COLESLAW

¼ green cabbage, shredded

¼ red cabbage, shredded

½ red onion, thinly sliced

1 carrot, grated

½ yellow pepper, deseeded and thinly sliced

½ red pepper, deseeded and thinly sliced

pinch of chopped fresh coriander

4 tbsp olive oil

juice and zest of 1 lime

pinch of mild chilli powder

salt and pepper

1. Mix the vegetables and coriander together in a bowl. Add the oil, lime juice and zest and chilli powder and season. Stir until well mixed and coated, then adjust the flavourings to your liking.

2. Refrigerate until needed.

Sweet Potato WEDGES

8 small sweet potatoes, washed, skin on

2 tbsp olive oil

1 tsp smoked paprika

salt and pepper

1. Preheat the oven to 200°C/180°C fan/400°F/Gas mark 6.

2. Cut the potatoes into thick wedge shapes, tip into a bowl, drizzle over the oil and mix to coat. Sprinkle over the paprika and season.

3. Bake on a baking sheet for about 40 minutes until crispy.

Honey Glazed CARROTS

500g baby carrots, peeled

1 tbsp olive oil

2 tsp honey

salt and pepper

handful of chopped fresh parsley

1. Preheat the oven to 190°C/170°C fan/375°F/Gas mark 5.

2. Cook the carrots in boiling water for 5 minutes until tender. Drain, transfer to a baking tin and mix with the oil and honey. Season.

3. Roast for 25 minutes, then scatter with the parsley to serve.

cont...

Garlic BREAD

1 good-quality baguette

180g butter, at room temperature

2 garlic cloves, finely chopped

handful of flat-leaf parsley, finely chopped

salt and pepper

1. Preheat the oven to 190°C/170°C fan/375°F/Gas mark 5.

2. Cut an incision across the baguette, making sure you don't cut all the way through. Repeat at 3cm intervals.

3. Mix the other ingredients together in a bowl and spread it between the gaps.

4. Bake, wrapped in foil, on a baking sheet for 12 minutes, then remove the foil and cook for another 5 minutes until crispy.

Orange CUMIN RICE

450ml vegetable stock

1 tsp ground cumin

zest of ½ orange

200g basmati rice, washed

1 tbsp butter, softened

handful of chopped fresh coriander, to garnish

1. Bring the stock, cumin and orange zest to a boil, then add the rice and cook according to packet instructions.

2. Once cooked, allow to cool for 5 minutes, then fluff the rice with a fork.

3. Stir through butter and top with the coriander to serve.

cont...

Easy
SWEET PASTRY KIT

Base INGREDIENTS

Pastry:

Pack ready-made puff pastry

Washes:

1 egg, beaten, or 25g caster sugar mixed with 200ml water in a pan over a low heat until dissolved, then cooled

Icing Glaze:

150g icing sugar mixed with 2 tbsp milk to form a loose paste (add the milk gradually to reach a consistency you like)

100g sugar and 30g ground cinnamon, mixed together

handful of raisins

1 tbsp butter, cubed

Cinnamon RAISIN WHIRLS

1. Roll out the puff pastry into a thin rectangle and cover it with most of the cinnamon sugar mixture. Sprinkle the raisins over, then dab squares of butter in a staggered line down the length of the pastry.

2. Roll up lengthways into a long sausage, seal the seam with a little eggwash, then cut into slices that form spiral disc whirly things!

3. Brush each whirl with a little beaten egg, sprinkle on a little more cinnamon sugar mix and bake until golden brown.

4. When cool, zigzag some icing over and allow to set.

cont...

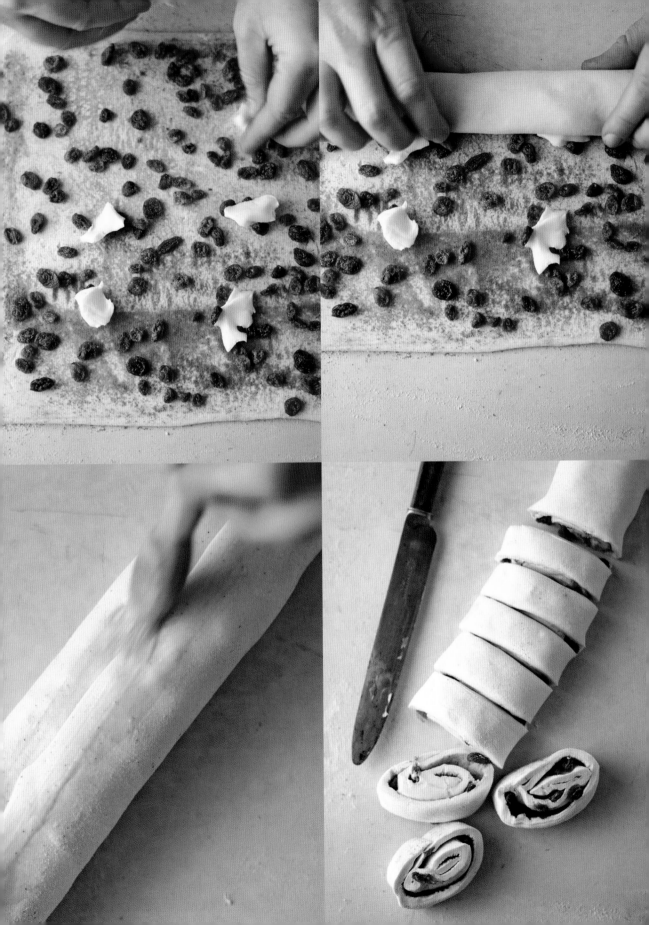

50g pecans, chopped

3 tbsp maple syrup

2 tbsp caster sugar

1 tbsp light cream cheese

Maple PECAN PLAIT

1. Blend together the pecans, maple syrup, caster sugar and cream cheese.

2. Cut the pastry into a rectangle shape, then, working lengthways across the pastry, cut a third of the way into the width of the pastry, making a diagonal incision backwards all along the length until you reach the end. Spin the dough around and repeat in the same direction along the width again. It should look like a sort of ribcage in pastry (sounds weird I know!) with diagonal strips and an area in the middle untouched all the way along – about one-third of the total width of the rectangle. Onto the untouched area place the chopped pecan filling.

3. Layer the diagonal strips over the filling alternately, like a braid, and tuck in at the ends, cutting off any excess.

4. Brush with some icing wash (see page 232), then bake until golden brown and top with some more icing.

cont...

stewed apple (homemade or from a tin)

store-bought custard

sultanas

sprinkling of ground cinnamon or nutmeg

Apple & SULTANA WINDMILL

1. Cut the pastry into a square shape, then make an incision from each corner to the centre of the pastry – but don't go all the way to the centre, stop 4cm from the centre (it should look like the letter 'X' that's not joined together). This little area in between the 'X' that is left is where you will put the filling.

2. Spoon the custard, then the apple mixture into the middle of the pastry, then sprinkle on the sultanas and the cinnamon and nutmeg.

3. When cutting the pastry you would have formed 4 little sections, so now fold each section in half to create a triangle but join the point into the apple mixture centre rather than going over – if you do this to all 4 sections, taking the triangle from the same side each time, it'll look like a windmill.

4. Brush the pastry with egg, then bake in the oven until golden. Once cool, drizzle over some icing sugar glaze(see page 232).

cont...

strawberry jam

peach slices (tinned or fresh)

lime zest

Peach & STRAWBERRY SQUARES

1. Cut the pastry into a square shape (you pick the size, depending on your appetite!).

2. Brush all around the edge of the square with beaten egg or sugar glaze – about 1½cm in will do it.

3. Spoon on the jam, then sit slices of peach in the jam, slightly overlapping each other.

4. Bake in the oven until the edges of the pastry have risen and are golden brown. When cool, dust icing sugar over and sprinkle with some lime zest.

Barry's Tips

I've done my best to describe the steps above to make these designs, but fear not, I've made a video recipe with Phoebe that shows the steps too. Check it out on my website or message me and I'll send you a link.

After brushing with egg you can sprinkle on some caster sugar for a crunchy sugar topping.

Use different ingredient combinations: nuts, jams, spreads, fruits, and lemon, lime and orange zests all work really well.

Bake the pastries in the oven according to the packet instructions, but keep your eye on them – they can burn quickly if you get complacent! Always bake on a tray lined with baking parchment to make it easier to remove the pastries.

Try not to overbake or the pastries will get too dry; sometimes you can be too keen for a golden top and the rest of the dough will harden up. Using the washes on page 232 should help prevent this and speed up the browning.

INDEX
ACKNOWLEDGEMENTS

Index

Acknowledgements

This book would not have been possible without the input, advice, support, belief and inspiration of so many people – some of whom I have listed below.

Thank you Mrs Barry (Becky!) for making this happen; dealing with the late nights and the late cooking; being a rock and bringing two amazing daughters into my life.

Thanks to Phoebe and Chloe for making me smile each day and kicking me in my man bits when putting you in the baby carrier.

Thanks to my family – Mum and Tony (and my dog Emmie!), Kristina and Tom, Charlene and Chris, Dick, Lesley and James – for putting up with me!

Thanks to Daniel and Sean Costello, Sean Mahon, Cindy Eisner (my American 'mom'), Samantha Marcone (my American sister), Nicole and Stephen Bossieux for being amazing friends.

Thank you to Jamie Oliver for inspiring me to start this journey and being a pucker (can I say that?!) chap, plus some of his cool colleagues who have all helped me in some way: Zoe Collins, Richard Herd, Ashley Day, Emily Taylor, Will Kinder, Matt Shaw, Jen Cockburn, Christina Mackenzie, Danny McCubbin and Jo Ralling.

Thanks also to Charlie Hart, Toby Quartley, Barry Smith, Helen Marriott, John McKenna, Barry and Patricia Crook for incredible advice and ongoing support. The two J's (Jonathan Conway and Jonny McWilliams) for all your help in this crazy new industry – I won't forget that mad day in London.

Thank you to HarperCollins for believing in me, wanting to share my story and be part of the journey, plus filling a room with the most people I have ever seen in 10 seconds! Anna Valentine, Carole Tonkinson, Georgina Mackenzie, Martin Topping, James Empringham, Orlando Mowbray, Laura Lees to name just a few.

Thanks also goes to Joanna Farrow, Judi Erde, Rebecca Rauter, Rob Allison, Nikki Morgan, Jessica Mills and Paula Johnson – food legends –for making sure I'm not poisoning anyone, and not forgetting Myles New, Tom Regester and Tony Hutchinson – Brill photography and props chaps, 'come on fashion boy', gert lush coffee, 'my mind's telling me no' etc.

Thanks to Desmond Grundy, Tamsin Wright and Brakeburn for the cool styling.

Thank you to some fun foodies I've met along the way so far: Bini Ludlow, Carl Pendle, Alex Lathbridge, Matt Kell, Selina Wragg, Martin Harte, Christian Stevenson, Kerryann Dunlop, Jemma Wilson and Paul Treyvaud as well as good friends who keep me level headed and owe me a beer for putting their names here: Mark and Sophie Caperton, Gary Bobbett, Ali Mills, Nats and Zak Pring, James and Lorna Mawditt (and Daisy!), Ed Studham, and John and Michelle Clark. Just a few of the many work chums at Wates who made an English guy welcome in Wales: Richard Leyshon (The Fox), Craig Stephens, Chris Bowen, Deb Bolton, Darren Powell, Martin Barnfield, Laura Bigmore, Robert Farrow, Deb Thomas, Matt McDaniel, Hazel Harris, Lisa Bailey.

And last but not least thanks to my lovely growing community of subscribers and followers on YouTube, Facebook, Twitter and Instagram for your ongoing support and interaction. You have, and continue to, play a huge part in doing what I do – thanks so much.

Get in touch!

I'd love to hear how you get on with my recipes.
You can contact me through any of the links below.
Speak to you soon!

www.myvirginkitchen.com
@myvirginkitchen.com
www.youtube.com/user/myvirginkitchen
instagram.com/myvirginkitchen

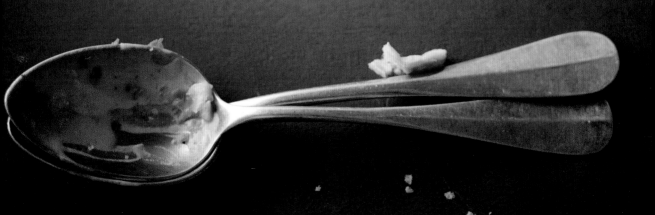